D1593179

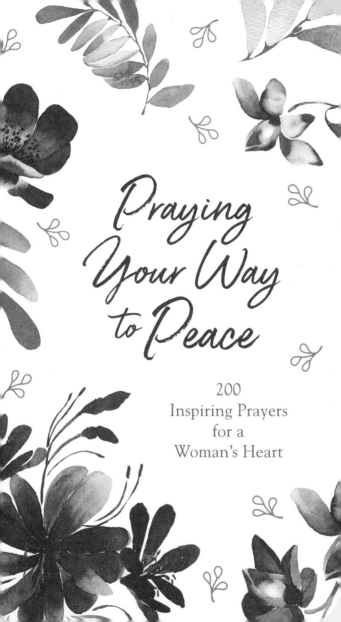

Praying Your Way to Peace

200 Inspiring Prayers for a Woman's Heart

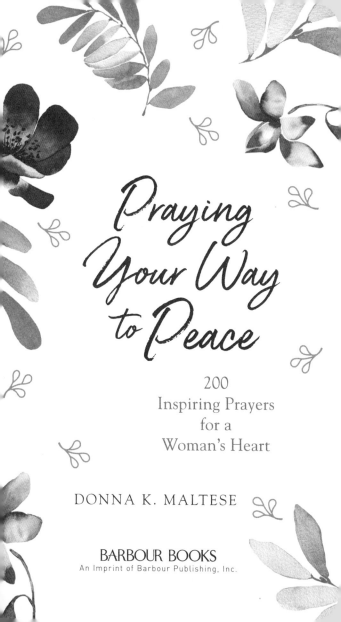

Praying Your Way to Peace

200
Inspiring Prayers
for a
Woman's Heart

DONNA K. MALTESE

BARBOUR BOOKS
An Imprint of Barbour Publishing, Inc.

© 2020 by Barbour Publishing, Inc.

ISBN 978-1-64352-496-2

Published by Barbour Books, an imprint of Barbour Publishing, Inc., 1810 Barbour Drive, Uhrichsville, Ohio 44683, www.barbourbooks.com.

Our mission is to inspire the world with the life-changing message of the Bible.

Printed in China.

Trusting Confidence

Thus said the Lord God, the Holy One of Israel: In returning [to Me] and resting [in Me] you shall be saved; in quietness and in [trusting] confidence shall be your strength. . . . And your ears will hear a word behind you, saying, This is the way; walk in it, when you turn to the right hand and when you turn to the left.

ISAIAH 30:15, 21 AMPC

These words are a reminder to me, Lord, of what I need to do, what I *want* to do, to have a good and peaceable life. I'm to return to You, to depend on You alone—not on fellow humans, animals, or machines. Only then will I find the true rest I need each day. Only then will my spirit find the quietness that feeds it, my soul the trusting confidence that nourishes it. As I rest and replenish myself in You, I find the strength to do what You've created me to do, to be who You created me to be. As I walk, Lord, direct my feet. Open my ears to Your Spirit's guidance every step of the way. Amen.

Tranquility of Heart and Life

*And the Lord said to Moses, Say to Aaron
and his sons, This is the way you shall bless the
Israelites. Say to them, The Lord bless you and watch,
guard, and keep you; the Lord make His face to
shine upon and enlighten you and be gracious (kind,
merciful, and giving favor) to you; the Lord lift up His
[approving] countenance upon you and give you peace
(tranquility of heart and life continually).*

NUMBERS 6:22–26 AMPC

I am so ready for peace, Lord. I'm tired of losing my
cool, of letting my emotions take over. So help me get
it through my head, Lord, that You are continually
blessing me. That You are guarding and taking care
of me no matter where I am or what I'm doing. That
Your face shines on me, if only I would just look up and
search for it. That You are kindness itself and overflow
with mercy. And that best of all, You are continually
giving me the peace that I crave, calming my heart
and my life. All I have to do is receive it. And that's
what I do in this moment, Lord, as I open my heart
and mind to You. Flood me with Your peace. Amen.

God Is Near

Rejoice in the Lord always [delight, gladden yourselves in Him]; again I say, Rejoice! Let all men know and perceive and recognize your unselfishness (your considerateness, your forbearing spirit). The Lord is near [He is coming soon]. Do not fret or have any anxiety about anything, but in every circumstance and in everything, by prayer and petition (definite requests), with thanksgiving, continue to make your wants known to God. And God's peace [shall be yours].

<small>PHILIPPIANS 4:4–7 AMPC</small>

More often than not, Lord, I find myself complaining about my lot in life, how hard it is just to survive sometimes. But moaning and groaning just bring me down even further. So I'm making it a point, Lord, to memorize and live these verses. To rejoice because You are with me. To let others see how gentle I am in You. To show them—and perhaps myself—that I know I never need worry or complain because You are with me. Because You are so near, as near as my next breath, I need not be anxious. Instead, I will pray to You, ask for what I need, and count on You to listen and provide. For then, and only then, will I have the peace I require and desire. Amen.

Filling Your Mind

Let petitions and praises shape your worries into prayers. . . . Before you know it, a sense of God's wholeness, everything coming together for good, will come and settle you down. It's wonderful what happens when Christ displaces worry at the center of your life. . . . You'll do best by filling your minds and meditating on things true, noble, reputable, authentic, compelling, gracious—the best, not the worst; the beautiful, not the ugly; things to praise, not things to curse.

PHILIPPIANS 4:6–8 MSG

The peace I feel in Your presence, Lord, is unfathomable. Abiding in You, my praises shape my worries into a prayer to You, the God of my life. I then expect and await Your peace to come down on me, to settle my heart, to calm my mind, to take the place of any lingering worries or frustrations. And then I make it my aim to be more aware of what I'm thinking about. To direct my thoughts so that I focus on the good in my life, the blessings from Your hand, the truth of Your Word, the comfort of Your presence, and the beauty of Your world. Thank You, Lord, for all these gifts and more. Amen.

The Angel of God Moved

Moses told the people, Fear not; stand still (firm, confident, undismayed) and see the salvation of the Lord which He will work for you today. For the Egyptians you have seen today you shall never see again. The Lord will fight for you, and you shall hold your peace and remain at rest. . . . And the Angel of God. . .moved. . . . And Israel saw that great work which the Lord did.

EXODUS 14:13–14, 19, 31 AMPC

Lord, You have vowed to help me, to protect, shield, and look out for me. So please give me the courage to stand still, to not run away from the battle but keep my eyes open as I wait for *You* to move on my behalf. I don't want to live a life of fear, be a complainer, or nervously pace the floor. I want to be calm, knowing You're surrounding me. To hold my peace, knowing You're the Prince of Peace. For just as Your angel moved to stand between the Israelites and the Egyptians, I know Your angel will move to stand on my behalf. Amen.

Unbroken Companionship

*The Lord [earnestly] waits [expecting, looking,
and longing] to be gracious to you; and therefore
He lifts Himself up, that He may have mercy on you
and show loving-kindness to you. For the Lord is a
God of justice. Blessed (happy, fortunate, to be envied)
are all those who [earnestly] wait for Him, who expect
and look and long for Him [for His victory, His favor,
His love, His peace, His joy, and His matchless,
unbroken companionship]!*

ISAIAH 30:18 AMPC

How wondrous is Your love for me, Lord. To think that
You are longing to be gracious to me. That You, the
Creator and Sustainer of the universe, are rising up
to show me the mercy and compassion You have for
me. As You look down, waiting for me, I'm looking up
to You. I am patiently waiting, expecting and longing
for You and all the blessings You have in store for me.
You have perfect timing, Lord. You know just what
to do and when to do it. So I'm leaning back on You,
fully confident in Your goodness and basking in Your
presence, loving Your peace and this sense of unbroken
companionship with and in You. Amen.

Strong and Courageous

"No one will be able to stand against you as long as you live. I will be with you, just as I was with Moses. I will not leave you or forsake you. Be strong and courageous. . . . Above all, be strong and very courageous to carefully observe the whole instruction My servant Moses commanded you. Do not turn from it to the right or the left, so that you will have success wherever you go."

JOSHUA 1:5–7 HCSB

When I hear or read words such as these, Lord, I realize I need not let my fears overwhelm me or even disturb me. Instead I'm to remember, believe, and trust Your Word is truth and power. Because You are with me, no one can stand against me. Just as You were with Moses and Joshua, You are also with me, here and now. So today, as I take up Your courage, my fears are banished. Your peace now reigns in their place. Unencumbered by worries and woes, I can finally breathe, stand firm, and walk where You would have me walk. In Jesus' name, amen.

The Peace of Me

"This book of instruction must not depart from
your mouth; you are to recite it day and night so that
you may carefully observe everything written in it.
For then you will prosper and succeed in whatever
you do. Haven't I commanded you: be strong and
courageous? Do not be afraid or discouraged, for the
LORD your God is with you wherever you go."

JOSHUA 1:8–9 HCSB

Throughout Your Word, Lord, You continually tell me to be strong and courageous. It's not just an idea or a polite request—You *command* this of me! So why is it sometimes so hard to do? Why do I too often feel weak and frightened? To grasp on to or lay claim to this strength and courage You offer, help me, Lord, to go deeper into this command. To meditate on it, memorize it, and melt it into my heart. Then once strength and courage become the very fabric of my being, lead me to the next words You would have me learn and memorize, until they fill me with peace. In Jesus' name, amen.

Already Endowed

The angel of GOD appeared to him and said,
"GOD is with you, O mighty warrior!" Gideon replied,
"With me, my master? If GOD is with us, why has
all this happened to us? . . . The fact is, GOD has
nothing to do with us—he has turned us over
to Midian." But GOD faced him directly:
"Go in this strength that is yours."

JUDGES 6:12–14 MSG

Some days, Lord, I'm so discouraged. So many things are happening in this world that are out of my control. So many things are keeping me up at night, as I wonder and worry about what may happen next. So many things seem to be so much bigger than me and my faith. So many things going wrong make me wonder where You are.

And then You appear in my mind. You whisper in my ear. You remind me that because You are with me, I will never be alone. You tell me to move forward in the strength You have spoken into my life, the strength that is now part of me, owned by me.

You alone give me peace and respite from the world's troubles, Lord. You alone are bigger than anything that can ever come against me. Help me, Lord, to take on the power, to assume the mantle of strength with which You've endowed me. In Jesus' name, amen.

The Least Granted Peace

Gideon said to Him, "O Lord, how can I save Israel?
See, my family is the least in Manasseh. And I am
the youngest in my father's house." But the Lord
said to him, "For sure I will be with you. . . ."
. . . And he said, "I am afraid, O Lord God!
For now I have seen the angel of the Lord face to
face." The Lord said to him, "Peace be with
you. Do not be afraid. You will not die."
JUDGES 6:15–16, 22–23 NLV

Sometimes, Lord, I feel as if I'm the least of all people.
That there is nothing about me that's of any value or
help to You. That I'm no one special. But then You
come along and tell me that no matter what *I* think
about myself, You have other ideas, plans for me. You
know I can do anything because *You are with me!* Help
me plant that fact in my heart and write it on the wall
of my mind. Because You are with me, I need not be
afraid. All I need to do is think of You, tap into Your
power, do what You call me to do, and take in Your
peace. Thank God! Amen.

Heart Pour, Peace Rich

*Hannah said, "Oh no, sir—please! I'm a woman hard
used. . . . The only thing I've been pouring out is my
heart, pouring it out to GOD. . . . It's because I'm so
desperately unhappy and in such pain that I've stayed
here so long." Eli answered her, "Go in peace.
And may the God of Israel give you what you
have asked of him." . . . She. . .went her way.
Then she ate heartily, her face radiant.*

1 SAMUEL 1:15–18 MSG

❧

Overwhelmed, I come to You, Lord. I've been picked
on, bullied, taunted, teased, and trampled. No one
understands the pain I'm feeling, except for You. So
it's to You I come. It's to You that I pour out my troubles, bare my soul, and bring my heartfelt desires. It
is before You that I get the relief I so crave. It's from
You that I receive the peace I need to rise up from
my knees and carry on. May You, Lord, my God, my
Beloved, my Prince, grant me what I have asked for,
what I long for. Be with me as I go on my way in You,
heart no longer heavy but filled with peace. In Jesus'
name, amen.

Sleep in Heavenly Peace

Answer me when I call, O my God Who is right and good! You have made a way for me when I needed help. Be kind to me, and hear my prayer. . . . You have filled my heart with more happiness than they have when there is much grain and wine. I will lie down and sleep in peace. O Lord, You alone keep me safe.

PSALM 4:1, 7–8 NLV

There are few things more precious than a good night's sleep. And that's just what I get when I put all my trust in You, Lord. When my head hits the pillow, before I know it, thoughts about the day echo in my mind. These thoughts are soon followed by what-ifs about tomorrow. But thinking about the future rarely helps me relax and fall asleep. Thus, when what-ifs approach, I allow them to pass me by. I begin thinking about how You continually pave a way for me to walk. How You lift me up and out of trouble—or walk with me through it. And that's all I need, to find You surrounding me, shielding me from harm. It is then I find my blessed peace. In Jesus' name, amen.

Peacemaker

Blessed. . . .are the makers and maintainers of peace,
for they shall be called the sons of God! . . . If when you
are offering your gift at the altar you there remember
that your brother has any [grievance] against you, leave
your gift at the altar and go. First make peace with your
brother, and then come back and present your gift.
MATTHEW 5:9, 23–24 AMPC

Some people in this world can be so contentious, Lord.
They are divided on many different levels. Many seem
to want to pick a fight instead of choosing to reach
out in peace, to hurt instead of help, to harm instead
of heal, to hate instead of love. Lord, I want to be a
peacemaker. I want to be the one to see what I have
in common with others instead of pointing out our
differences. To help instead of harm, love instead of
hate. But I'll need Your help. Show me, Lord, where I
can help others like You've helped me. Show me how I
might exude comfort instead of conflict. Let me begin
by making peace with the brother or sister I've harmed,
and then come back and offer myself to You. Amen.

A Picture of Peace

Like an apple tree among the trees of the wood, so is my
beloved [shepherd] among the sons [cried the girl]! . . .
[I can feel] his left hand under my head and his right
hand embraces me! . . . [Vividly she pictured it]
The voice of my beloved [shepherd]! . . . Arise,
my love, my fair one, and come away.

SONG OF SOLOMON 2:3, 6, 8, 13 AMPC

❧

You, Lord, are my pathway to peace. I look to You.
I picture You lying beside me. When I close my eyes
and imagine You here with me, I can feel Your left
hand under my head, Your right hand embracing me,
pulling me close to Your warmth and love, giving me
the comfort I long for. And as I lie here, totally content, amazingly calm, I know nothing can harm me.
Nothing can worry or dismay me. For I not only feel
Your presence but hear Your voice telling me You love
me. That You will continually protect and guide me.
That because of You in my life, I need not complain,
worry, or fear. Thank You, Lord, for this picture of
peace. Amen.

Perfect and Constant Peace

You will guard him and keep him in perfect and constant peace whose mind [both its inclination and its character] is stayed on You, because he commits himself to You, leans on You, and hopes confidently in You. So trust in the Lord (commit yourself to Him, lean on Him, hope confidently in Him) forever; for the Lord God is an everlasting Rock [the Rock of Ages].

ISAIAH 26:3–4 AMPC

There are very few certainties in life, and that's why I am so glad You've called me, Lord! I trust in You to keep me safe and sound, to hear when I call to You, and to guide me along the way. It is because of my confidence in You, Abba God, that my mind has such perfect peace. For I know You alone stand between me and danger. My hope rests in You alone. So all the troubles in this world, all the things that seem so challenging, I'm putting in Your hands—and leaving them there! For I know nothing can stand up against You, my solid Rock, Friend, and beloved Companion. My perfect peace. Amen.

My Beloved Shepherd

[So I went with him, and when we were climbing the rocky steps up the hillside, my beloved shepherd said to me] O my dove, [while you are here]. . .in the sheltered and secret place of the cliff, let me see your face, let me hear your voice; for your voice is sweet, and your face is lovely. [My heart was touched and I fervently sang to him my desire] Take for us the foxes, the little foxes that spoil the vineyards [of our love].

SONG OF SOLOMON 2:14–15 AMPC

In Your company, my Beloved, I can climb to the highest of heights. You keep me safe and secluded in Your secret place. It's here You ask me to let You see my face and hear my voice. Just the fact that You'd like to do those things, to listen to me and love me, brings me so much joy. So I am ready to raise my voice to You in song, Lord. Allow me to stay in You, walk with You, climb with You. And to rest in You, confident You will remove anything that threatens to come between us. In Jesus' name, amen.

A Great and Wonderful Calm

*They. . .awakened Him, saying, Lord, rescue and
preserve us! We are perishing! And He said to them,
Why are you timid and afraid, O you of little faith?
Then He got up and rebuked the winds and the sea,
and there was a great and wonderful calm (a perfect
peaceableness). And the men were stunned with
bewildered wonder and marveled, saying,
What kind of Man is this, that even
the winds and the sea obey Him!*

MATTHEW 8:25–27 AMPC

When I'm in the middle of a storm, Lord, I know that
because of Your presence, because You are riding out the
storm with me, I have nothing at all to worry about. I
have nothing at all to fear. After all, You have already
rescued me from death. You have already overcome
all evil. So all I need to do is remain confident that
You are in control of the situation. That You will, at
just the right moment, rise up and tame the wind and
waves assailing me. That You will take this tumultuous
situation and bring into it a great and wonderful calm.
And I will once more stand before You and marvel.
Amen.

"All Is Well"

The child sat on her lap till noon, and then he died.
And she went up and laid him on the bed of the man
of God and shut the door behind him and went out. . . .
She said, "All is well." . . . When the man of God saw
her coming, he said to Gehazi his servant. . . "Run at
once to meet her and say to her, 'Is all well with you?
Is all well with your husband? Is all well with the
child?'" And she answered, "All is well."

2 KINGS 4:20–21, 23, 25–26 ESV

There is something wonderful as well as disturbing in the story of the Shunammite woman, Lord. Even after her son dies, she keeps saying, "All is well." It's wonderful that she can remain that calm during such a heart-wrenching account. Yet at the same time, it's a bit disturbing that she does. What cool! What calm! Yet that's just the kind of peace I want, Lord. So help me to remember that with You living with me and in me, I too can have this woman's confidence. I too can have peace within even when it seems as if all is falling apart without. In Jesus' name, amen.

Go in Peace

She. . .came up behind him in the crowd and touched his garment. For she said, "If I touch even his garments, I will be made well." And immediately the flow of blood dried up. . . . Jesus, perceiving in himself that power had gone out from him, immediately turned about. . . . "Daughter, your faith has made you well; go in peace, and be healed of your disease."

MARK 5:27–30, 34 ESV

Here I am, Lord, coming up behind You, hoping to touch You, knowing, being certain that when I do, Your power will transform my situation. How or in what way, I do not know. Neither do I know when, whether You'll change things up today or tomorrow. Nor do I know where You will work Your way, here or somewhere else. Yet none of that really matters. Just having such faith in You makes me feel better. Knowing that You, who does all things well, will move on my behalf allows me to place this problem in Your hands and go my way, in Your way of peace. Amen.

Opened Eyes

An army with horses and chariots was around the
city. Elisha's servant said to him, Alas, my master!
What shall we do? [Elisha] answered, Fear not;
for those with us are more than those with them.
Then Elisha prayed, Lord, I pray You, open his eyes
that he may see. And the Lord opened the young
man's eyes, and he saw, and behold, the mountain
was full of horses and chariots of fire.

2 KINGS 6:15–17 AMPC

Lord, I feel like I'm surrounded by chaos. I'm overwhelmed, feeling hemmed in, as if there's no way
out. That I have done all that I can do. But this is a
battle I can no longer fight. So it is to You that I turn
for help, for a solution, for hope. And as I turn my
thoughts to You, as I lay my problem at Your feet, I
hear Your voice, Your words telling me not to fear. You
are more than able to protect me from all things, all
people—even from my own self, doubts, and negative
thoughts. You alone make it clear that I need never
worry because there is no force more powerful than
You. With opened eyes, I find my joy, my peace, my
renewed hope and vision in You. Amen!

Because of You

Standing behind Him at His feet weeping, she began to wet His feet with [her] tears; and she wiped them with the hair of her head and kissed His feet [affectionately] and anointed them with the ointment (perfume). . . . He said to her, Your sins are forgiven! . . . Your faith has saved you; go (enter) into peace [in freedom from all the distresses that are experienced as the result of sin].

LUKE 7:38, 48, 50 AMPC

Jesus, You know I'm not perfect. Yet You still accept me, love me, help me, and understand me when I come before You. If I could, I would fall at Your feet, wet them with my tears of joy, wipe them with my hair, anoint them with perfume, and cover them in kisses. For because of You and what You did on the cross, my sins have been forgiven and forgotten. Because of You, I can come boldly before Father God and speak to Him. Because of You, I can have peace of mind and freedom from stress. Because of You, I have a life I want to live and yet surrender to You. What a God I serve! Amen!

In a Nutshell

*Rejoice in the Lord always. . . . Let your reasonableness
be known to everyone. The Lord is at hand; do not be
anxious about anything, but in everything by prayer and
supplication with thanksgiving let your requests be made
known to God. And the peace of God, which surpasses
all understanding, will guard your hearts and your
minds in Christ Jesus. Finally. . .if there is anything
worthy of praise, think about these things. What you
have learned and received and heard and seen
in me—practice these things, and the
God of peace will be with you.*

PHILIPPIANS 4:4–9 ESV

You, Lord, are the answer to my problem. As they
have before and will continue to do, Your words provide the remedy to my wretchedness. Looking from
my pain to Your pleasure, I raise my thoughts to You
and in praise of You. Because You are so close, I need
fear nothing. Instead, I bring my silent thank-Yous
and pleas to You alone, heart to heart. As I do, I am
infused with Your peace. My mind reels in all good
things and casts out the not-so-good things. I watch,
listen, learn, and practice from the saints before me.
In a nutshell, I abide in You. Amen!

The Soul Child Within

Lord, my heart is not haughty, nor my eyes lofty;
neither do I exercise myself in matters too great or in
things too wonderful for me. Surely I have calmed and
quieted my soul; like a weaned child with his mother,
like a weaned child is my soul within me [ceased
from fretting]. O Israel, hope in the Lord
from this time forth and forever.

PSALM 131:1–3 AMPC

Father God, I have put aside any grandiose plans I may have had for myself. I don't get caught up in things that are way beyond my comprehension. Instead, I have put myself and my future in Your hands. I tackle the things You call me to do, follow the plans You have made for me, walk on the path You have laid out for me. I live and breathe in Your rhythm. In doing so, I have transformed my heart within to be calm. No outside or inside noises can shake me. I no longer fuss, fear, or fret. My soul is like a weaned child within me. I am in Your hands, held close with love because of Your Son, in whose name I pray. Amen.

The Lord Is Peace

And when Gideon perceived that He was the Angel of the Lord, Gideon said, Alas, O Lord God! For now I have seen the Angel of the Lord face to face! The Lord said to him, Peace be to you, do not fear; you shall not die. Then Gideon built an altar there to the Lord and called it, The Lord is Peace. To this day it still stands.

JUDGES 6:22–24 AMPC

Lord, You are not an abstract apparition. You are a true, living supernatural being, one whom people have seen face-to-face and heard heart to heart. You have created me, have formed my shape, have whispered to me as I lay curled up inside my mother's womb, and have brought me forth into this world. You are the part of my being that guides me and hides me. You are my Lord of peace. It is to You I turn, Your voice of encouragement I count on, Your light I look for, Your peace I crave. So be with me now, Lord, as I lift my eyes to You, the One who still stands. Hold me close as I shelter beneath Your arms and breathe freely. Amen.

A Way Follower

"Blessed be GOD, who has given peace to his people Israel just as he said he'd do. Not one of all those good and wonderful words that he spoke through Moses has misfired. May GOD, our very own God, continue to be with us just as he was with our ancestors—may he never give up and walk out on us. May he keep us centered and devoted to him, following the life path he has cleared, watching the signposts, walking at the pace and rhythms he laid down for our ancestors."

1 KINGS 8:56–58 MSG

My beloved and blessed God, there is no promise You have spoken that You have not also fulfilled. Everything You told Moses would happen happened. You and Your words give me rest from all sides, all quarters, all factions within and without. They are my life and breath. Not only are Your words truth, but they also have the power to calm me, to settle me down and make me content. So continue to be with me, Lord. Don't give up on me but keep me with You, centered, a follower of Your way. Amen.

A Better Place

*These mentioned by name were princes in their families;
and their fathers' houses increased greatly [so they
needed more room]. And they journeyed to the entrance
of Gedor. . .to seek pasture for their flocks. And they
found rich, good pasture, and the [cleared] land was
wide, quiet, and peaceful, because people of Ham
had dwelt there of old [and had left it a better
place for those who came after them].*

1 Chronicles 4:38–40 AMPC

We seem, Lord, to be living in an era during which a perfect storm is attacking somewhere every day. Sometimes that storm takes the shape of a tornado, hurricane, earthquake, tsunami, flood, drought, famine, war—you name it. Perhaps if we'd taken better care of the earth, a responsibility You gave us in the beginning, these storms wouldn't be happening. But they are. So, Lord, help me be the kind of woman, the kind of caring being, who leaves this world a better place than she found it. To further that end, Lord, show me how You would have me nurture our earth and, in turn, Your people. In Jesus' name, amen.

The Path of Peace

You, my child, "Prophet of the Highest," will go ahead
of the Master to prepare his ways, present the offer of
salvation to his people, the forgiveness of their sins.
Through the heartfelt mercies of our God, God's Sunrise
will break in upon us, shining on those in the darkness,
those sitting in the shadow of death, then showing us
the way, one foot at a time, down the path of peace.

LUKE 1:76–79 MSG

You, Lord, are the sunrise of my life. Because of Your
mercy and love, Your light can and does shine on
me. You take me by the hand and lead me out of the
darkness of confusion. You muffle the world's noise
and begin singing a love song to me alone. You bring
me into the light of Your being where I am forgiven
but not ever forgotten. Thank You, Lord, for these
blessings. Thank You for the way You patiently nurture
and encourage me, whispering Your promise never
ever to let go. And most of all, Lord, thank You
for leading me down the path of Your peace, one slow
step at a time. Amen.

"Child, Arise!"

*Someone from the ruler's house came and said,
"Your daughter is dead; do not trouble the Teacher
any more." But Jesus on hearing this answered him,
"Do not fear; only believe, and she will be well." . . .
Taking her by the hand he called, saying, "Child,
arise." And her spirit returned, and she got up
at once. And he directed that something
should be given her to eat.*

LUKE 8:49–50, 54–55 ESV

Sometimes, Lord, I slip into fear mode so easily. And soon after, I'm not just frightened but in a panic! That's no way to go through life. So here I am before You once more, Lord. You tell me, "Do not fear; only believe." For when I do, all You have promised will become a reality—*my* reality. Take me by the hand and help me rise up once more. Help me to get back onto Your path, ready to follow Your direction, to go where You lead. For guided by You, I know I'll find my way to the peace that overcomes all fear. With You in my life, in me, around me, above and below me, all will be well. In Jesus' name, amen.

My Inner Self

Have mercy on me and be gracious to me, O Lord,
for I am weak (faint and withered away); O Lord,
heal me, for my bones are troubled. My [inner] self
[as well as my body] is also exceedingly disturbed and
troubled. But You, O Lord, how long [until You
return and speak peace to me]? Return [to my relief],
O Lord, deliver my life; save me for the sake
of Your steadfast love and mercy.

PSALM 6:2–4 AMPC

When I am in distress, faint and withering away, come to me, Lord. Heal my body. Give me the physical and mental strength of body and mind that I need to do Your will, to follow Your lead. Calm the storm within my mind, spirit, and heart. Speak words of comfort to my soul. Show me within Your Book the words of peace and love I need to hear, words that will blossom within me, transforming me, helping me to grow more and more into the likeness of Your Son, my Master. Deliver me from myself and pull me up into Your kingdom and grace. In Jesus' name I pray. Amen.

Boomerang

*Go your way; behold, I send you out like lambs into
the midst of wolves. . . . Whatever house you enter,
first say, Peace be to this household! [Freedom from all
the distresses that result from sin be with this family].
And if anyone [worthy] of peace and blessedness is
there, the peace and blessedness you wish shall come
upon him; but if not, it shall come back to you.*
LUKE 10:3, 5–6 AMPC

What a wonderful way to spread Your peace, Lord,
by taking it on the road. You have a direction for me
to take. A path to follow. My job and joy are to trust
and follow Your leading. So show me, Lord, where
You would have me go, which household You would
have me reach out to. Then give me courage to enter
into the unknown there and to bless that household
with Your peace. . . . Yet if Your peace and blessing
are neither wanted nor warranted by that household,
I thank You for setting things up so that the peace and
blessedness I wish upon others will come back upon
me. That's a boomerang result I'll never dodge. Amen!

Still Waters

*The Lord is my Shepherd [to feed, guide, and shield me],
I shall not lack. He makes me lie down in [fresh, tender]
green pastures; He leads me beside the still and restful
waters. He refreshes and restores my life (my self);
He leads me in the paths of righteousness [uprightness
and right standing with Him—not for my
earning it, but] for His name's sake.*

PSALM 23:1–3 AMPC

I am just a little lamb, Lord, oftentimes scared and in need of a leader, a protector, a guide. That is why You, Lord, are my all in all. You, as my Shepherd, feed me. You guide me as we walk through the wilderness, over mountain and plain, across city streets and boulevards. With You leading me, being with me, watching over my life, I find I lack for nothing. When I need rest, You have me lie down in green meadows. When I need refreshing and restoring, within and without, You guide me to still waters. You lead me down all the right paths—not because I deserve it, Lord, but so that I can glorify You today and every day. Amen.

Courage and Comfort

Though I walk through the [deep, sunless] valley of the shadow of death, I will fear or dread no evil, for You are with me; Your rod [to protect] and Your staff [to guide], they comfort me. You prepare a table before me in the presence of my enemies. You anoint my head with oil; my [brimming] cup runs over. Surely or only goodness, mercy, and unfailing love shall follow me.

PSALM 23:4–6 AMPC

Too often, Lord, fear creeps into my life, leaving me feeling unsettled, off-kilter. And there are so many things to be afraid of on this side of heaven, in this world. But fear has no place, no foothold in Your world, Lord. So, please, Abba God, help me get from this world to Yours. Help me reenter that place, that valley where, even though things may look scary, I know they're not—because You're there, with me in the midst of both shadows and sunlight. You're the One whose rod protects me, fending off any and all attackers. Your staff is the device that guides me, leading where You'd have me go. It is in You alone, Lord, that I find not just courage and comfort but goodness, love, and mercy—everything a little lamb could want. Amen.

Open Doors

By entering through faith into what God has always wanted to do for us—set us right with him, make us fit for him—we have it all together with God because of our Master Jesus. . . . We throw open our doors to God and discover at the same moment that he has already thrown open his door to us. We find ourselves standing where we always hoped we might stand—out in the wide open spaces of God's grace and glory, standing tall and shouting our praise.

ROMANS 5:1–2 MSG

Because of my faith in You, Jesus, I am just where our Father God wants me—right with Him. I now have not just peace with God but access to Him! I've thrown open my door to my Creator only to discover that at that exact same moment, He's thrown His door open to me! There is now nothing between us! No barrier to keep me from my all-powerful Provider, my beloved Lord, and one and only Master, Yahweh! In this I rejoice! In Jesus' name, amen.

Even Then

The Lord is my Light and my Salvation—whom shall I
fear or dread? The Lord is the Refuge and Stronghold of
my life—of whom shall I be afraid? . . . Though a host
encamp against me, my heart shall not fear; though war
arise against me, [even then] in this will I be confident.
One thing have I asked of the Lord, that will I seek,
inquire for, and [insistently] require: that I may
dwell. . .[in His presence] all the days of my life.

PSALM 27:1, 3–4 AMPC

You, Lord, are the One who divided the Red Sea,
stopped the sun, and sent chariots of fire to protect
Your prophet. Throughout the ages, You've continually proven Yourself to be the God of all gods! Thus,
with You on my side, I need have no fear. In fact, I
am calm. For there's no one who can outdo You, God
Almighty. Even if I'm caught in a war, *even then* I'll
be at peace within because You're here to help me, to
pull me into Your safety net. Continue to be with me,
Lord, loving me, holding me, calming me all the days
of my life, to the end. Even then. Amen.

A Plain and Even Path

In the day of trouble He will hide me in His shelter; in the secret place of His tent will He hide me; He will set me high upon a rock. . . . Although my father and my mother have forsaken me, yet the Lord will take me up [adopt me as His child]. Teach me Your way, O Lord, and lead me in a plain and even path.

PSALM 27:5, 10–11 AMPC

When trouble comes, hide me, Lord. Shelter me in Your secret place, high up, way beyond the reach of those who want to harm me. And in that place, Lord, give me the wisdom I need to regain my footing. Remind me that, although members of my family, friends, and others I have known may abandon me, *You* will never do so. For You are my Abba. You've adopted me into Your family. What comfort, what peace I find in knowing that I will never be alone, that I will always have You. So, Lord, walk me down that plain and even path I share with You. Amen.

In the Land of the Living

Your face (Your presence), Lord, will I seek,
inquire for, and require. . . . [What, what would have
become of me] had I not believed that I would see the
Lord's goodness in the land of the living! Wait and hope
for and expect the Lord; be brave and of good courage
and let your heart be stout and enduring. Yes,
wait for and hope for and expect the Lord.

PSALM 27:8, 13–14 AMPC

❧

I seek You and Your face, Lord. I search for Your wisdom. I require Your presence. For You alone get me through the hard days. You alone give me the peace I need amid the battle. You alone give me the courage to face another hour, day, week, month. When things get very difficult, Your Word gives me the hope I need to carry on. I don't know what would have become of me if I had not anticipated, expected, and watched for Your goodness in the land of the living. For You, Lord, I wait with courage and hope with great expectation. In Jesus' name, amen.

Cuddled and Coddled

"You have been helped by Me before you were born and carried since you were born. Even when you are old I will be the same. And even when your hair turns white, I will help you. I will take care of what I have made. I will carry you, and will save you. . . . I am God, and there is no other. I am God, and there is no one like Me."

ISAIAH 46:3–4, 9 NLV

It's hard to imagine, Lord, that You helped me *before I was even born*—and that *since* then, You continued to carry me, looking out for me, watching over me, and helping me. That in itself gives me a great sense of peace. But further, You tell me that even when I'm old and gray, You'll still be there. You'll still carry me and rescue me. Ah, what sweet calm flows over me. How wonderful to know I'm still a babe in Your arms. I'm still someone who is and desires to be cuddled and coddled. It's true: there is no one like You, Daddy God. For that I am ever grateful! Amen.

Standing Word

*"I tell from the beginning what will happen in the end.
And from times long ago I tell of things which have not
been done, saying, 'My Word will stand. And I will do
all that pleases Me.' I call a strong and hungry bird from
the east, the man from a far country who will do what
I have planned. I have spoken, and I will make it
happen. I have planned it, and I will do it."*

ISAIAH 46:10–11 NLV

Lord, it's amazing how well Your Bible books fit together. How the Old Testament supports the New.
How the psalms soothe minds, bodies, souls, and spirits
unlike any other book. How the Gospels tell Your
story with four different audiences in mind. How the
letters to the New Testament churches tell us how to
live, and how Jesus' revelation tells us what to expect
when He returns. Lord, Your Word not only stands
but transforms—people as well as circumstances. What
You have said, You *will* make happen. What You have
planned, You *will* do. Help me to rest in the peace of
that promise, Lord. Speak to me, tell me what part You
would have me play in Your plan. In Jesus' name, amen.

Quieting Down

Open up before GOD, keep nothing back; he'll do whatever needs to be done: He'll validate your life in the clear light of day and stamp you with approval at high noon. Quiet down before GOD, be prayerful before him. Don't bother with those who climb the ladder, who elbow their way to the top. Bridle your anger, trash your wrath, cool your pipes—it only makes things worse. Before long the crooks will be bankrupt; GOD-investors will soon own the store.

PSALM 37:5–9 MSG

I can't take it, Lord. Nor do I understand it. Why do those who are evil have the best lives? They seem to have everything they could ever want or need while so many believers, like me, struggle every day just to survive. Yet You tell me not to worry about those who step on other people to get ahead in this world. So. . .I won't. Instead of ranting at the prosperity of evildoers, I'm going to quiet down before You, settle into Your peace. Because I know that, in the end, all those who follow You alone will have the true reward: a place in eternity with You. In Jesus' name I pray. Amen!

Freeing Up

Take heed to yourselves and be on your guard, lest your hearts be overburdened and depressed (weighed down) with. . .worldly worries and cares pertaining to [the business of] this life. . . . Keep awake then and watch at all times [be discreet, attentive, and ready], praying that you may have the full strength and ability and be accounted worthy to escape all these things [taken together] that will take place, and to stand in the presence of the Son of Man.

LUKE 21:34, 36 AMPC

I need Your help, Lord. I'm getting so weighed down by the news of what's happening in the town and country I live in and beyond. It's so depressing. Yet I'm pretty sure I wasn't made to take on all the troubles of this world. My frame wasn't built to bear the weight of that load. So help me, Lord, to turn my eyes from troubles and focus on You. Give me the words to pray when I hear bad news from any quarter—local or foreign. Tell me how to help humans, animals, and nature. Help me stay awake and aware of You so that I will have the strength to do Your will. In Jesus' name, amen.

God Will Not

Let your character or moral disposition be free from love of money [including greed, avarice, lust, and craving for earthly possessions] and be satisfied with your present [circumstances and with what you have]; for He [God] Himself has said, I will not in any way fail you nor give you up nor leave you without support. [I will] not, [I will] not, [I will] not in any degree leave you helpless nor forsake nor let [you] down (relax My hold on you)! [Assuredly not!]

HEBREWS 13:5 AMPC

A concern about contentment has come up for me, Lord. Because lately I find myself more focused on my finances than on my faith. It's not that I love money. It's that I'm worried I won't have enough to make ends meet. I think that maybe I'll be okay for today, but chances are I'll be floundering tomorrow. Remind me, Lord, that my allegiance and focus are to be on You alone, not on my lack of money. Remind me that no matter what shape my finances are in, You'll never fail me, give me up, or abandon me. You will not in any way, shape, or form ever leave me without support. You'll never release Your hold on me or leave me helpless. You are my peace. Amen.

Forever the Same

The heavens are the work of Your hands. They shall
perish, but You shall remain and endure; yes, all of
them shall wear out and become old like a garment.
Like clothing You shall change them, and they shall be
changed and pass away. But You remain the same,
and Your years shall have no end. . . . Jesus Christ
(the Messiah) is [always] the same, yesterday,
today, [yes] and forever (to the ages).
PSALM 102:25–27; HEBREWS 13:8 AMPC

Your creation surrounds me, Lord. Your mountains, skies, creeks, grass, earth, birds, wind, rain, snow, sun, stones, stars, bunnies, and deer are continually changing, shifting, transforming. Someday they may fall aside, fade out, blow away, and be forever gone. It's quite unsettling, being caught in a world of continual change. Yet then I think of You and realize that although creation may change, You the Creator never will. You are a forever God. Through Jesus You have opened the gateway to eternity, have made a way for me to live with You. So today I rest in the peace of the unchangeable You, both now and forever. Amen.

A Happy Woman of Peace

*The steps of a [good] man are directed and established
by the Lord when He delights in his way [and He busies
Himself with his every step]. Though he falls, he shall
not be utterly cast down, for the Lord grasps his hand
in support and upholds him. . . . Mark the blameless
man and behold the upright, for there is a
happy end for the man of peace.*

PSALM 37:23–24, 37 AMPC

What a relief, Lord! The idea that You direct my steps
makes me feel so content. Because if You're delighting
in my way and walking with me, I know I can have
peace about today and tomorrow. For You are with
me with each step I take. And even if I trip up or fall,
You'll pull me back up onto my feet! You, Lord, are
my main support. You are what motivates me, drives
me, comforts me, and secures me. Thank You, Lord,
for always being here for me, for making me a happy
woman of peace in You. Amen.

Getting a Grip

There's one other thing I remember, and remembering, I keep a grip on hope: GOD's loyal love couldn't have run out, his merciful love couldn't have dried up. They're created new every morning. How great your faithfulness! I'm sticking with GOD (I say it over and over). He's all I've got left. GOD proves to be good to the man who passionately waits, to the woman who diligently seeks.

LAMENTATIONS 3:21–25 MSG

Some days, Lord, it seems relatively easy to lose hope. The problems to be tackled seem to be growing by the minute. It's enough to make even the strongest of believers despair! But I'm leaning into You, Lord. I'm remembering how every morning with You is a new beginning. Because You have unlimited mercy and love, You create them new every morning! That's how faithful You are to me even when I might hesitate to be faithful to You! Forgive me, Lord, for my missteps. For You are my all in all, my greatest hope, my everlasting love. I will continue to seek You and adore You always, for in You I find my peace. Amen.

Enter the Silence

*It's a good thing to quietly hope, quietly hope for help
from God. It's a good thing when you're young to stick
it out through the hard times. When life is heavy and
hard to take, go off by yourself. Enter the silence.
Bow in prayer. Don't ask questions: Wait for hope
to appear. Don't run from trouble. Take it
full-face. The "worst" is never the worst.*
LAMENTATIONS 3:26–30 MSG

It's been a long few days, Lord. And I need some time
away with You. Some time to sit quietly and tap into
Your power and grace, to reacquaint myself with Your
Word and the hope I find there. I need to step back,
step away from the daily grind, even if only for a moment. Perhaps only for this very moment. Right here,
right now, Lord, I come to You. I enter the silence, and
I bow in prayer. Here I await Your blessing of hope,
confidence, courage, and trust. In Jesus' name I wait
and pray. Amen.

An Abundance of Peace

For yet a little while, and the evildoers will be no more; though you look with care where they used to be, they will not be found. But the meek [in the end] shall inherit the earth and shall delight themselves in the abundance of peace. . . . Better is the little that the [uncompromisingly] righteous have than the abundance [of possessions] of many who are wrong and wicked.

PSALM 37:10–11, 16 AMPC

It's good to know, Lord, that the good guys will eventually win out over the bad ones. That at some point, those who have carried out evil plans, those who've harmed themselves or others, will one day have their comeuppance. That someday the meek will end up inheriting the earth and delighting in a wealth of peace on earth. In the meantime, Lord, help me keep my eyes on You, live a "right" life, and leave all the judgment of others to You. Help me obey You at every crossroad, turn where You'd have me turn, do what You'd have me do. To be as my Jesus, meek and gentle yet firm and strong. In His name I pray. Amen.

Blast from the Past

*One thing I do: Forgetting what is behind and reaching
forward to what is ahead, I pursue as my goal the
prize promised by God's heavenly call in Christ Jesus.
Therefore, all who are mature should think this way.
And if you think differently about anything, God will
reveal this also to you. In any case, we should
live up to whatever truth we have attained.*

PHILIPPIANS 3:13–16 HCSB

Too often, Lord, my past encroaches upon then disrupts my present. The mistakes I had once made, the consequences that followed, keep reverberating in my head. That sometimes makes it difficult for me to keep my focus on You, the present, and what You'd have me do in the moments that make up a day. So help me, Lord, to find my peace by forgetting what has happened before, what cannot be undone, and then help me reach forward to what lies ahead of me as I follow after You. Show me, Lord. Reveal Yourself and Your plan to me. Point out to me the way You'd have me go as I blast away from the past. Amen.

Standing By

The Lord stood by me and strengthened me, so that
through me the [Gospel] message might be fully
proclaimed and all the Gentiles might hear it. So I was
delivered out of the jaws of the lion. [And indeed] the
Lord will certainly deliver and draw me to Himself from
every assault of evil. He will preserve and bring me
safe unto His heavenly kingdom. To Him be the
glory forever and ever. Amen (so be it).

2 TIMOTHY 4:17–18 AMPC

❧

People come and go throughout my life, but You, Lord,
are always here with me. You're the One standing by
me, giving me the courage to do what You've called
me to do. You give me the confidence to stand my
ground, to face whatever comes against me. Because
You've delivered me in the past, I know You'll do it
in the present and future. Best of all, Your presence
of light and love reminds me that even if things don't
go the way I think they should, all is and will be well
because You have the best plan for me. In all this I
find an undefinable and undeniable peace. Amen.

Beneath the Wings

*He who dwells in the secret place of the Most High
shall remain stable and fixed under the shadow of the
Almighty [Whose power no foe can withstand]. I will
say of the Lord, He is my Refuge and my Fortress,
my God; on Him I lean and rely, and in Him I
[confidently] trust! . . . He will cover you with
His pinions, and under His wings shall
you trust and find refuge.*
PSALM 91:1–2, 4 AMPC

There is a place like no other. It is here I find You.
In the silence, in the smile of a child, the call of a
bird, the rustle of a leaf, the smell of rain, I am swept
away to another time and place in You. It is here
that I can truly breathe. It is in Your presence that
I find the warmth, light, and calm I need to repair
and recharge. It is in this secret place that I can find
my feet, knowing I'm secure beneath the wings of
the Almighty. Hold me here, Lord, my Refuge and
Fortress. Give me the love, peace, and strength I need
to find and walk Your way today. Amen.

Supernatural Protection

*Because you have made the Lord your refuge, and the
Most High your dwelling place, there shall no evil befall
you, nor any plague or calamity come near your tent.
For He will give His angels [especial] charge over you
to accompany and defend and preserve you in all your
ways [of obedience and service]. They shall bear you up
on their hands, lest you dash your foot against a stone.*

PSALM 91:9–12 AMPC

The idea of angels watching over me is so precious,
Lord. Yet it's not just an idea—it's a *reality*. Because
I have made You my safe place, You've given Your
angels charge over me. You've sent them to walk
with me, take care of me, and protect me in all I do.
They've been instructed to hold me up in their hands
so I don't stumble and fall when the road gets rough.
You as my safe place. . .supernatural protection. . .a
sure refuge—all these things lead to peace and to You,
Lord, my Provider of peace. Amen.

Personal Knowledge

*Because he has set his love upon Me, therefore will I
deliver him; I will set him on high, because he knows
and understands My name [has a personal knowledge
of My mercy, love, and kindness—trusts and relies
on Me, knowing I will never forsake him, no, never].
He shall call upon Me, and I will answer him;
I will be with him in trouble, I will deliver him.*

PSALM 91:14–15 AMPC

The more I learn about You, Lord, the more I love You.
The more I understand what You have done for me,
the more I trust You. There are, of course, some things
I may never know, but I'm okay with that because I
have confidence in You for not just one or two things
but for *all* things. I trust that You have a plan for me.
That You will answer my call if ever I'm in trouble.
That You will come to me and be with me in the *midst*
of trouble. That You will never let me go. Because with
You and me, Lord, it's personal. What love, what peace,
what protection I have in You! Amen.

Great Things Await

"Do not be distressed or angry with yourselves because
you sold me here, for God sent me before you to
preserve life. . . . God sent me before you. . .to keep
alive for you many survivors. So it was not you
who sent me here, but God. He has made me
a father to Pharaoh, and lord of all his house
and ruler over all the land of Egypt."

GENESIS 45:5, 7–8 ESV

When I'm lying awake at night wondering, *Why me?*
or *What did I do to deserve this?* I inevitably come back
to Joseph. All the things that he'd been through—
sold to slave traders by his brothers, unjustly accused
of a crime, thrown into a dungeon, then forgotten
and neglected—would be enough to crush such a
dreamer, to turn his stomach into a knot of anxiety
and frustration. But instead, Joseph stuck with God,
stayed calm, and carried on, continually going on to
the next thing, knowing that God was in control and
that great things awaited him! That's how I want to be,
Lord. As calm, cool, and collected as Joseph, during
good times and bad. Amen.

My Safe Place

*After these things, the word of the Lord came to Abram
in a special dream, saying, "Do not be afraid, Abram.
I am your safe place. Your reward will be very great."
. . . The Lord showed Himself to Isaac. . .and said,
"I am the God of your father Abraham. Do not be
afraid, for I am with you. I will bring good to you."*

Lord, I need to keep Your formula in mind. That when
I come to You, put all my trust and confidence in You,
and make You my safe place, then I find good, a reward.
You appeared to two famous fathers—Abram and
Isaac—and made sure they knew they had no reason
to be afraid. You were their safe place. Because You
were very present in their lives, they knew the road to
peace within. That's the road I want to become very
familiar with, Lord. I want to get to a place where, no
matter what happens, I remain unruffled in You. Lead
me on, Lord. Amen.

Nothing Lost

Jesus then took the loaves, and when he had given
thanks, he distributed them to those who were seated.
So also the fish, as much as they wanted. And when
they had eaten their fill, he told his disciples, "Gather up
the leftover fragments, that nothing may be lost."
So they gathered them up and filled twelve baskets
with fragments from the five barley loaves
left by those who had eaten.

JOHN 6:11–13 ESV

Lord, You are continually amazing me with Your power, wisdom, and creativity, all of which shine through the stories in Your Word. Each day, I reach for Your Book and find a new lesson, a new treasure, a new phrase that draws me closer to knowing You. Today I'm reminded of how well You provide for me, how prayers and faith move me in the telling and doing, and then move You to provide a miracle, to go beyond a point I thought unreachable. Today I find my peace knowing that You, Lord, are the ultimate Provider, the God of wonder, the Spirit of light. Thank You for never allowing anything to be lost. Even me. Amen.

The Right Shore

*They saw Jesus walking on the sea and approaching
the boat. And they were afraid (terrified). But Jesus
said to them, It is I; be not afraid! [I Am; stop being
frightened!] Then they were quite willing and glad for
Him to come into the boat. And now the boat went
at once to the land they had steered toward. [And
immediately they reached the shore toward which
they had been slowly making their way.]*

JOHN 6:19–21 AMPC

Sometimes, Lord, I wonder why I'm getting nowhere
with a project, task, challenge, or situation. I feel as
if I'm out on a stormy sea, unable to see past the wind
and waves, that all my rowing, all my efforts to move
things forward are coming to naught. And then I
realize I haven't invited You into my plans. For some
reason, I've left You out of my equation. So here I
am, Lord, letting You into my plan. Here's what I'm
steering toward. Now that we're together on this, I
can ride on in peace and make my way to the right
shore with You. Amen.

Live Carefree

*All of you, leaders and followers alike, are to be down
to earth with each other, for—God has had it with
the proud, but takes delight in just plain people. So be
content with who you are, and don't put on airs.
God's strong hand is on you; he'll promote
you at the right time. Live carefree before
God; he is most careful with you.*

1 PETER 5:5–7 MSG

Lord, I want to be down-to-earth, talking straight not
only to other humans but to You too. But I'll need Your
help. Please give me the courage to tell You everything
that's happening in my life; the things I've thought,
said, and done; the good, the bad, and the ugly. I want
not just to be satisfied, content with who I am, but
to be assured that You too are content, perhaps even
happy, with who I am or the woman I'm working toward being. But most of all, Lord, I want to turn over
to You *all* the things that are bothering me, give You
all my burdens, my fumes and frets, and leave them in
Your more than capable hands. In Jesus' name, amen.

Even Better

*Fear not, for I have redeemed you [ransomed you by
paying a price instead of leaving you captives]; I have
called you by your name; you are Mine. When you pass
through the waters, I will be with you, and through the
rivers, they will not overwhelm you. When you walk
through the fire, you will not be burned or scorched,
nor will the flame kindle upon you. For I am the Lord
your God, the Holy One of Israel, your Savior.*

Isaiah 43:1–3 ampc

Oh Lord, You give me such peace of mind. When I
am afraid, You tell me to "fear not" because You've
redeemed me, even though it cost the sacrifice of Your
Child. And You continue to reach out for me, willing
and longing to help me. You've even called me by
name, claiming ownership of me—mind, body, and
soul. Even better, You've promised to stick with me
through times of fire and times of rain. And all because
You love me, all because You want me in Your world,
Your presence. Alleluia, amen!

Unshaken

God is our safe place and our strength. He is always our
help when we are in trouble. So we will not be afraid,
even if the earth is shaken and the mountains fall into
the center of the sea, and even if its waters go wild with
storm and the mountains shake with its action. . . .
God is in the center of her. She will not be moved.
God will help her when the morning comes.

PSALM 46:1–3, 5 NLV

You, Lord, are my center. Because You are standing
solidly within me, I need not be moved. Nothing can
shake me unless I allow it to. Help me to keep this in
mind, Lord. To remember that I have You as my source
of strength, courage, and hope. You alone are my safe
place. You are always there when I'm in trouble no
matter what that trouble is. So I will not be afraid. Even
if the earth is shaken to its core, I will stand strong. I
will remember I am Your child, Your daughter. And
that You will help me when the daylight breaks and
beyond. Amen.

Let Be, Be Still, and Know

The Lord of hosts is with us; the God of Jacob is our Refuge (our Fortress and High Tower). . . . Let be and be still, and know (recognize and understand) that I am God. I will be exalted among the nations! I will be exalted in the earth! The Lord of hosts is with us; the God of Jacob is our Refuge (our High Tower and Stronghold). Selah [pause, and calmly think of that]!

PSALM 46:7, 10–11 AMPC

I awaken with the words *be still and know* echoing in my mind. Reading them, hearing them, a supernatural calm drifts down upon me. Knowing that my God, the gentle Shepherd who leads me, is also my high tower, impenetrable fortress, eternal refuge, and lion tamer fills me with delight and wonder. I marvel at how an almighty God can also be so gentle, how a Master can be a servant. And then I hear You call my name. I turn and there You are, with me. Filled with Your presence, I let everything go. I empty my body of all tension and my mind of all thoughts but these: *Let be, be still, and know that I am God.* And soon Your surpassing peace reigns. Amen.

The Secret of Facing Every Situation

*Not that I am implying that I was in any personal
want, for I have learned how to be content (satisfied
to the point where I am not disturbed or disquieted)
in whatever state I am. I know how to be abased and
live humbly in straitened circumstances, and I know
also how to enjoy plenty and live in abundance.
I have learned in any and all circumstances
the secret of facing every situation.*
PHILIPPIANS 4:11–12 AMPC

❧

Help me get it through my head, Lord, that I, by myself, cannot meet my own needs. That only through
You can I find the true contentment, joy, and peace
I crave. Instead of trying to come up with my own
solutions or thinking I know better than You, I'm
going to trust You for everything—big and small. I'm
going to allow You into every facet of my life. And
I'm going to be satisfied with who I am, what I have,
and where I am as I keep my eyes on You. For I know
You do all things well and in Your own time. In You,
I am content with all. Amen.

God's Planning

*Joseph replied, "Don't be afraid. Do I act for God?
Don't you see, you planned evil against me but
God used those same plans for my good, as you see
all around you right now—life for many people.
Easy now, you have nothing to fear; I'll take
care of you and your children." He reassured
them, speaking with them heart-to-heart.*

GENESIS 50:19–21 MSG

Lord, the news—local and international—is full of
reports of people acting from their worst instincts
and ideas. Such events are more than unsettling.
Yet this behavior, people hurting people, has been
happening for thousands of years, hasn't it? Still, I
cannot get used to it. When others hurt, so do I.
We're all connected, all Your people. So, Lord, help
me gain some peace about this. Give me the courage
to adopt Joseph's attitude—to remember that even
while others plan evil, You can use those same plans
for my good and the good of others. Because that's
what You do, I know I really have nothing to fear,
nothing to worry about, no reason to hold a grudge.
Ah, that's how I find peace—Your peace as You turn
evil into good. Thank God! Amen.

Peace of Knowledge

*I have learned in any and all circumstances the secret
of facing every situation, whether well-fed or going
hungry, having a sufficiency and enough to spare or
going without and being in want. I have strength for all
things in Christ Who empowers me [I am ready
for anything and equal to anything through Him
Who infuses inner strength into me; I am
self-sufficient in Christ's sufficiency].*

PHILIPPIANS 4:12–13 AMPC

No matter what's happening in my life, Lord, I know
that because of You, I'll never want for anything.
For I belong to You, the master Creator, Maintainer,
and Sustainer of all things. And because I'm Yours,
everything I see around me reminds me of You, Your
power, Your beauty, and Your love. All I have, want,
and require is in You, from You, and through You.
Because I live in You and Your Son, I have it all, including strength to do, think, or say what You would
have me do, think, or say. Through Your Son I'm ready
for anything because He is my everything, my security,
strength, and peace. In Jesus' name, amen.

A Good Place

*I cried to the Lord in my trouble, and He answered me
and put me in a good place. The Lord is with me. I will
not be afraid of what man can do to me. The Lord is
with me. He is my Helper. I will watch those lose who
fight against me. It is better to trust in the Lord
than to trust in man. It is better to trust in
the Lord than to trust in rulers.*

PSALM 118:5–9 NLV

God, You are not just "my strength and my song"
(Psalm 118:14 NLV); You are my peace. You are the
One who calms my racing heart, caresses my weary
brow, and holds my shaking hand. Whenever I'm in
trouble, You hear my call. You realize what's happening, answer my SOS, lift me up, and put me in a good
place. A place where You are. When You are with me,
Lord, I'm not afraid. When You are with me, when I'm
conscious of Your presence, I realize I have all I need.
Unlike humans, You can be trusted, Lord. With and
in You, I find my good place. Amen.

Do Not Let

Do not let your hearts be troubled (distressed, agitated).
You believe in and adhere to and trust in and rely on
God; believe in and adhere to and trust in and rely also
on Me. . . . Believe Me that I am in the Father and
the Father in Me; or else believe Me for the sake of
the [very] works themselves. [If you cannot trust
Me, at least let these works that I do in
My Father's name convince you.]

JOHN 14:1, 11 AMPC

Lord, I'm having trouble maintaining my peace. That may be because my attention has shifted. For during these tumultuous times, I'm more focused on the world's troubles than I am on You. And that's never a good tack to take. So help me get back on the right line, Lord. Bring back to my mind all the things You have done—in history and in my life. Show me the world through Your eyes. Guide me in how to make my priorities those of heaven, not earth. Remind me, God, of who You are—the Father I trust, the Son I lean on, and the Spirit I seek. Amen.

Relax

*"'Daniel,' he said, 'man of quality, listen carefully
to my message. And get up on your feet. Stand at
attention. I've been sent to bring you news.'
When he had said this, I stood up, but I was still
shaking. 'Relax, Daniel,' he continued, 'don't be
afraid. From the moment you decided to humble
yourself to receive understanding, your prayer
was heard, and I set out to come to you.'"*

DANIEL 10:11–12 MSG

I'm amazed, Lord, at how often You and Your angels
tell me not to fear. And yet even faith-filled believers
like Daniel sometimes shook with fright. I'm pretty
certain I too would shake in fear if an angel came to
visit me. So I'm feeling a bit better about the qualms
that sometimes wiggle their way into my life, mind,
heart. Even so, it's good to hear the words *relax and
don't be afraid.* It's nice to be reminded that You *answer*
prayers. That You hear me when I call and then send
out an angel to help me. In this moment, Lord, open
my ears to Your voice, my eyes to Your light, my heart
to Your peace, and my spirit to Your angels. Amen.

A Place for You

*In My Father's house there are many dwelling places
(homes). If it were not so, I would have told you;
for I am going away to prepare a place for you.
And when (if) I go and make ready a place for you,
I will come back again and will take you to Myself,
that where I am you may be also. And [to the
place] where I am going, you know the way.*

JOHN 14:2–4 AMPC

I like it, Lord, that You're a Man with a plan. That
You have been with me since the beginning, are still
with me now, and will be with me in the future. Yet
it's not just that truth that keeps me calm and content.
It's the fact that Father God has a nice home waiting
for me. And that You have gone ahead to prepare that
place for me—for me alone. To me, Lord, this isn't
just a place in the future but a place I can visit now.
A place where I can be with You alone. A place of
peace, comfort, and hope. A place of light and love.
A place of never-ending choruses of amens.

Lambs in Arms

"Look! Your God!" Look at him! GOD, the Master,
comes in power, ready to go into action. He is going to
pay back his enemies and reward those who have loved
him. Like a shepherd, he will care for his flock, gathering
the lambs in his arms, hugging them as he carries them,
leading the nursing ewes to good pasture.

ISAIAH 40:10–11 MSG

Lord, You are the giver, the bringer, the gatherer, the lover, the leader of life. You are the source of all power and light. And to the ones who love You, You come in power and take action. You, my champion and Good Shepherd, care for me in every stage of my life—from lamb to ewe and all the phases in between. And as You care for and love me, Your light and warmth cover me, enclose me, protect and caress me. I find my true peace, my haven, when I imagine Your strong and steady arms embracing me. Continue to lead me along Your pathway. Ease me into Your will and desire. Show me how to maintain my peace in Your pasture. And my eyes will continue to look to You, my God, my Master, my Shepherd. Amen.

Princess of Peace

*If anyone steadfastly believes in Me, he will himself
be able to do the things that I do; and he will do even
greater things than these, because I go to the Father.
And I will do [I Myself will grant] whatever you ask
in My Name [as presenting all that I Am], so that
the Father may be glorified and extolled
in (through) the Son.*

John 14:12–13 AMPC

You have promised, Jesus, that all who believe in You
can do the things You could do—and that they will
do even greater things! Attached to that promise is
another, that whatever we ask Father God for, if we
ask it in Your name, our request will be granted. I have
total faith in You, Jesus, in Father God, in the Spirit,
and in the power You all wield. And as a believer, I
come to my Prince of Peace: Lord, make me a princess
of peace. Help me find calm when I come into Your
presence. Help me maintain that calm assurance when
I step out into my day. Then at night, Lord, help me
rest myself in peace as I close my eyes, lean back against
Your chest, and whisper, "Good night, sweet Prince
of Peace." Amen.

"Return to Me"

"I have made you, you are My servant. O Israel, I will not forget you. I have taken away your wrong-doing like a dark cloud, and your sins like a fog. Return to Me, for I have bought you and set you free." . . . The Lord, Who makes you, bought you and saves you, and the One Who put you together before you were born, says, "I am the Lord, Who made all things."
ISAIAH 44:21–22, 24 NLV

Some days, Lord, I'm amazed that You want me, that You want me to return to *You*. But You do! You've said that You, the One who has made me, will not forget me. That all the things I've done wrong, all the mistakes I've made—knowingly or unknowingly—You have taken away. They are no more. They're like a fog that's here then gone. Once more, I am amazed that You can obliterate my missteps like that. My one request today is that You help *me* forget my missteps and mistakes. Help me forgive myself for hurting You and anyone else who felt the results of my wrongdoing. Then, only then, will I have true peace in Jesus' name. Amen.

The Standby

I will ask the Father, and He will give you another
Comforter (Counselor, Helper, Intercessor, Advocate,
Strengthener, and Standby), that He may remain with
you forever—the Spirit of Truth, Whom the world
cannot receive (welcome, take to its heart), because it
does not see Him or know and recognize Him.
But you know and recognize Him, for He lives
with you [constantly] and will be in you.
I will not leave you as orphans.

JOHN 14:16–18 AMPC

Sometimes, Father, I feel just like an orphan, "comfortless, desolate, bereaved, forlorn, helpless" (John 14:18 AMPC). I've lost so many people in my life that I feel more alone than ever. I take comfort in the fact that the three-in-one person I have not lost and will never lose is You, Your Son, and Your Spirit. You have promised that Your Spirit will live with me forever. Your envoy will comfort, advise, help, intercede, advocate, strengthen, stand by me. He, that amazing Spirit of truth, is just the remedy I need to keep me from feeling all alone. He gives me peace of mind, heart, soul, and spirit. With You all as my true and forever family, I am eternally blessed. In Jesus' name, amen.

Desired Haven

Some go down to the sea and travel over it in ships. . . . Then they cry to the Lord in their trouble, and He brings them out of their distresses. He hushes the storm to a calm and to a gentle whisper, so that the waves of the sea are still. Then the men are glad because of the calm, and He brings them to their desired haven.

PSALM 107:23, 28–30 AMPC

Troubles are causing a storm within and without, Lord. My calm has been shaken, my thoughts disrupted. I'm truly not sure what to do. And then, in desperation, I cry out to You. Immediately I feel relief, just in sharing my troubles with You, the One who knows me best. You hush the storm within, and I feel a gentle calm come over me. I can now hear Your whisper where a howling gale once surrounded me. The tumultuous waves have even become still. In this glad state, this state of peace, I feel sane and safe once more. You have brought me back to You, my desired haven in the best and worst of times. For no time is wasted in Your peace, Your presence. My God, You are my shelter from all storms. Amen.

Moving In

*"I'm in my Father, and you're in me, and I'm in you.
The person who knows my commandments and keeps
them, that's who loves me. And the person who loves
me will be loved by my Father, and I will love him and
make myself plain to him. . . . If anyone loves me,
he will carefully keep my word and my Father will
love him—we'll move right into the neighborhood!"*

JOHN 14:20–21, 23 MSG

I have a sense of peace within me each time I think
of You, Jesus. I feel so complete knowing You are
in God, I'm in You, and You're in me. Because that
means that no matter where I am or what I'm doing,
I'm never alone. I always have someone with me who
can give me wisdom, lift me up, shelter me from harm,
and love me like no other. The last on that list is the
most important, Lord, because this world can be such
a loveless, unforgiving place. Fortunately for me, Lord,
You loved me before I even knew You. That's a love to
treasure, to count on, to rest in. Thank You. Amen.

Replenish

*Lift up your eyes on high and see! Who has created
these? . . . Have you not known? Have you not heard?
The everlasting God, the Lord, the Creator of the ends
of the earth, does not faint or grow weary; there is no
searching of His understanding. He gives power to
the faint and weary, and to him who has no
might He increases strength [causing it to
multiply and making it to abound].*
ISAIAH 40:26, 28–29 AMPC

I know who You are, Lord. You're the Creator of all.
The One who holds, maintains, and sustains the entire
world. I have known this. I had heard about it. But
sometimes, almost unknowingly, I forget who You are
. . .and, for that matter, who *I* am! I get so caught up
in the day-to-day machinations in this world that I
put You and Your power, strength, and knowledge to
the side and tap into my resources alone. That's when
I get into trouble. So here I am, Lord, faint and weary.
Replenish me with Your peace, power, and strength.
Shower me with Your wisdom. And help me keep my
mind on You every moment of the day. Amen.

Within Me

Peace I leave with you; My [own] peace I now give and bequeath to you. Not as the world gives do I give to you. Do not let your hearts be troubled, neither let them be afraid. [Stop allowing yourselves to be agitated and disturbed; and do not permit yourselves to be fearful and intimidated and cowardly and unsettled.]

JOHN 14:27 AMPC

It's strange reading the words "Stop allowing yourselves to be agitated and disturbed; and do not permit yourselves to be fearful," for I rarely consider that I have control over these things. And yet I do. I have a choice to make. I can allow the events of my day and my reactions to them to break my peace or not. I choose: not. But I will need Your help, Lord, to hang on to Your peace. The one You left with me. The very peace You carried, have given to, and bequeathed to me. To hang on to Your peace, I'm going to spend more time in You, with You, attending to You, beginning today by reminding myself over and over again that the God of peace is within me. Amen.

The Spirit Takes Flight

Even youths shall faint and be weary, and [selected]
young men shall feebly stumble and fall exhausted;
but those who wait for the Lord [who expect, look for,
and hope in Him] shall change and renew their strength
and power; they shall lift their wings and mount up
[close to God] as eagles [mount up to the sun];
they shall run and not be weary, they shall
walk and not faint or become tired.

ISAIAH 40:30–31 AMPC

I am weary, Lord, doing too much too often in too little time. And then I come to You. And time stops as I wait on You. I begin in Your Word, expecting and looking for hope, wisdom, and direction. Then I close my eyes and fall into Your realm. It's there I can truly rest and renew myself, allowing Your energy and strength to fill my mind, body, heart, and soul. Soon I am lifted up as my spirit takes flight and soars its way into Your presence and lands at Your feet. Finally. Together with my Lord. Where there is no greater peace. In Jesus' name, amen.

The Good Shepherd's Voice

*I am the Good Shepherd; and I know and recognize
My own, and My own know and recognize Me. . . .
The sheep that are My own hear and are listening to
My voice; and I know them, and they follow Me.
And I give them eternal life, and they shall never lose
it or perish throughout the ages. [To all eternity
they shall never by any means be destroyed.]*

JOHN 10:14, 27–28 AMPC

There was just something about You, Jesus, that attracted me. Perhaps it was Your truth in a world of half truths. Maybe it was the fact that You were both gentle and powerful. Or because You gave Your life for me. But then one day I heard Your Word, Your *voice*—and I was truly and forever hooked. Day after day, hour after hour, I kept coming back to know, hear, and learn more about You and Your ways. To this day, I can't seem to get enough. My beloved Jesus, thank You for shepherding me. For giving me eternal life. For giving my soul a craving for Your voice. In Your name I pray. Amen.

Continual Blessing

*I will bless the Lord at all times; His praise shall
continually be in my mouth. My life makes its boast in
the Lord; let the humble and afflicted hear and be glad.
O magnify the Lord with me, and let us exalt His name
together. I sought (inquired of) the Lord and required
Him [of necessity and on the authority of His Word],
and He heard me, and delivered me from all my fears.*

PSALM 34:1–4 AMPC

No matter what is happening in my life, in my world, it is You, God, that I bless. For You hear me when I pray. Your love and kindness, Your compassion and mercy are all-encompassing. You make my life worth living. For life is no life at all when I'm tied up in troubles, distressed by doubts, and frantic with fears. So I come to You. When I enter Your presence, Your light obliterates my problems, indecisiveness, and insecurities. They fade into nothingness. And all that remain are Your light, warmth, and love. This is why I seek You, serve You, celebrate You, and surrender to You. In Jesus' name, amen.

The True Path

If you've gotten anything at all out of following Christ,
if his love has made any difference in your life. . .then
do me a favor: Agree with each other, love each other,
be deep-spirited friends. Don't push your way to the
front; don't sweet-talk your way to the top. Put yourself
aside, and help others get ahead. Don't be obsessed with
getting your own advantage. Forget yourselves
long enough to lend a helping hand.

PHILIPPIANS 2:1–4 MSG

Sometimes, Lord, I feel like I'm living a life where it's all about me and what I want. Yet I know from Your Word and my experience that my true path to peace comes when I forget my own needs, plans, and desires—when I put myself aside long enough to help someone else. So help me do that, Lord. Help me find a way to agree with and love others. To be a friend who is sel*f*less, not sel*f*ish. To look out not just for my own interests but also for the interest of others. To find a way to live in peace—within and without. In Jesus' name, amen.

Strength and Stronghold

The Lord is my Strength and my [impenetrable] Shield; my heart trusts in, relies on, and confidently leans on Him, and I am helped; therefore my heart greatly rejoices, and with my song will I praise Him. The Lord is their [unyielding] Strength, and He is the Stronghold of salvation to [me] His anointed. Save Your people and bless Your heritage; nourish and shepherd them and carry them forever.

PSALM 28:7–9 AMPC

Lord, You are an awesome God. Your strength is solid, Your shield impenetrable. That's why I lean on You more than anyone or anything else in my life. I trust You to hear my cries when I pray. I trust You to respond immediately, to look my way, to help me find my path through the challenges of this life. I continually and expectantly look for You to move in my life, to bless me and nourish me. To save me—for I cannot save myself. My strength and protection only go so far, Lord. I need You to be my help, strength, shield, and Savior, from now until the end of time. You are my pathway to peace. Amen.

Peace to You!

Jesus came and stood among them and said, Peace to you! . . . Then Jesus said to them again, Peace to you! [Just] as the Father has sent Me forth, so I am sending you. And having said this, He breathed on them and said to them, Receive the Holy Spirit! . . . Eight days later His disciples were again in the house. . . . Jesus came, though they were behind closed doors, and stood among them and said, Peace to you!

JOHN 20:19, 21–22, 26 AMPC

Nothing and no one can come between You and me, Jesus. Not even closed doors can keep You out. At one point, You walked through walls to get to Your followers. And I know You'll walk through more than walls to get to me. All so that I can hear Your message of peace. In this moment, Lord, come and stand beside me. Allow words of peace to come from Your lips, the airy essence of peace to cover me, the power of peace to pour down upon me. In Your name I pray and receive Your peace. Amen.

Safe Place of Peace

When I was desperate, I called out, and GOD got
me out of a tight spot. GOD's angel sets up a circle of
protection around us while we pray. Open your mouth
and taste, open your eyes and see—how good GOD is.
Blessed are you who run to him. Worship GOD if you
want the best; worship opens doors to all his goodness.

PSALM 34:6–9 MSG

Even when I'm desperate, in dire straits, I still have
peace. For You, God, always make a way even when I
see no way. You see the benefits of all situations, the
silver lining of every cloud. So when I call out, You do
the next thing. You take the next step to help me get
through whatever obstacle or problem is blocking my
way. And You go even further by commanding Your
angel to form a wall of protection around me, keeping
me from all harm. So, with mouth and eyes open, I'm
going to taste and see how good You are, Lord. As I
run to You, knowing I'll reach my safe place in Your
peace, I do so with exhilaration and joy, wondering
how You're going to work things out. . .for me, in
You. Amen.

Promised, Predicted, and Proposed

This [very] night there stood by my side an angel of the God to Whom I belong and Whom I serve and worship, and he said, Do not be frightened, Paul! It is necessary for you to stand before Caesar; and behold, God has given you all those who are sailing with you. So keep up your courage, men, for I have faith (complete confidence) in God that it will be exactly as it was told me.

ACTS 27:23–25 AMPC

God, throughout the ages, You have sent Your angels to watch over those who trust in You, the heirs of salvation. You've sent them as protectors, messengers, encouragers, and defenders. And, Lord, although I cannot see these supernatural beings, I know they, like You, are right here with me. That is why I can hang on to my peace and courage—and use them to inspire peace and courage in others. Like Paul, no matter where I've come from, where I stand today, and what lies before me, I too can say, "I have faith (complete confidence) in God that it will be exactly as it was told me." Whatever You've promised, predicted, or proposed, dear Lord, will become reality. Thus, I have peace knowing Your Word is my truth. In Jesus' name I pray. Amen.

A Way of Worship

*Listen to me; I will teach you to revere and worshipfully
fear the Lord. What man is he who desires life and
longs for many days, that he may see good? Keep your
tongue from evil and your lips from speaking deceit.
Depart from evil and do good; seek, inquire for,
and crave peace and pursue (go after) it! The eyes
of the Lord are toward the [uncompromisingly]
righteous and His ears are open to their cry.*

PSALM 34:11–15 AMPC

These days, Lord, so many people are hurting others
because they're no longer careful with words, whether
those words are spoken, texted, tweeted, emailed,
snail-mailed, or quoted. But words do have power. So,
as I continue on my peace trail, I'm going to follow
Your direction to watch what I say. To make sure my
words are not just true but encouraging. To leave evil
behind and make it a point to do good each day. And
most of all, Lord, I'm going to make it my aim and
passion not just to rest in peace but to look for, crave,
and pursue it. That will be my way of worshipping
You here on earth and in heaven above. Amen.

Deep Peace

Jesus answered them, "Do you finally believe? In fact,
you're about to make a run for it—saving your own
skins and abandoning me. But I'm not abandoned.
The Father is with me. I've told you all this so that
trusting me, you will be unshakable and assured,
deeply at peace. In this godless world you will
continue to experience difficulties. But take
heart! I've conquered the world."

JOHN 16:31–33 MSG

Even though others may leave my side, Lord, I know
You'll always be there for me. When others scatter in
fear or hide behind their "I'm busy" facade, You are
still walking with me, giving me courage and a secret
place of power. When others make a run for it, I'll
know I'm not alone. For I have Your three-person
team—Father, Son, and Holy Spirit—looking out for
me, going before me, and protecting me from behind.
Because of my trust in You, I am unshakable. I'm deep
into peace knowing that even though things may be
difficult here, You have already overcome this world
and are waiting for me in the next. In You I find peace
and take heart. Amen.

Catching Your Breath

Is anyone crying for help? GOD is listening, ready to rescue you. If your heart is broken, you'll find GOD right there; if you're kicked in the gut, he'll help you catch your breath. Disciples so often get into trouble; still, GOD is there every time.

PSALM 34:17–19 MSG

Spirit of the Lord, troubles seem to be everywhere! Each day it seems harder and harder to maintain any kind of peace. Yet that's what You bring. But You cannot bring it if I don't cry out for it. So help me to be more willing to come to You and share my troubles. Help me to be humble enough to ask for and accept whatever help You can bring me. I cannot live this life on my own. Too often I need an advocate. One who can translate my thoughts, remove the stains on my heart, and relieve the weight on my soul. Come close, hold me tight, and heal this broken heart. Help me catch my breath. Be here every time. Bring Your peace, Your protection, Your love, Your healing, Your power, and Your strength. Amen.

Back in Step

*Acquaint now yourself with Him [agree with God
and show yourself to be conformed to His will] and
be at peace; by that [you shall prosper and great] good
shall come to you. Receive, I pray you, the law and
instruction from His mouth and lay up His words in
your heart. If you return to the Almighty [and submit
and humble yourself before Him], you will be built up.*

JOB 22:21–23 AMPC

❧

I've been looking for peace, Lord. Yet it seems so
elusive at times. And then I realize I am out of step
with You and that may be a part of this disconnect
I've been feeling. So here I am, Lord. I'm giving in
to You, allowing my will to be aligned with Yours. As
each minute, hour, and day passes, I'm going to be at
peace, knowing You are once more my lead in this
life. Your direction and words are going to be instilled
in my heart so that I in all ways—body, mind, and
spirit—will be one with You, Your Son, and Your Spirit.
In submitting to You, in serving You, in watching and
waiting for You, I am renewed in, empowered by, and
back in step with You. Amen.

Well and Whole

*I call to God; GOD will help me. At dusk, dawn,
and noon I sigh deep sighs—he hears, he rescues.
My life is well and whole, secure in the middle of
danger. . . . Pile your troubles on GOD's shoulders—
he'll carry your load, he'll help you out.
He'll never let good people topple into ruin.*

PSALM 55:16–18, 22–23 MSG

Lord, right now in this moment "my insides are turned
inside out; specters of death have me down. I shake
with fear, I shudder from head to foot. 'Who will give
me wings,' I ask—'wings like a dove?' Get me out of
here on dove wings; I want some peace and quiet.
I want a walk in the country, I want a cabin in the
woods. I'm desperate for a change from rage and stormy
weather" (Psalm 55:4–8 MSG). So, Lord, I'm calling
on You, certain You'll help me, hear me, and rescue
me. I know that even though I may find myself in the
middle of danger, I'm safe and secure within You. For
when I find You, my troubles slide off my shoulders
and onto Yours. I know You, God, are strong and can
carry my load. For this I thank You. Amen.

The Way of Peace

No one understands [no one intelligently discerns or comprehends]; no one seeks out God. All have turned aside; together they have gone wrong and have become unprofitable and worthless; no one does right, not even one! . . . Destruction. . .and misery mark their ways. And they have no experience of the way of peace [they know nothing about peace, for a peaceful way they do not even recognize].

ROMANS 3:11–12, 16–17 AMPC

ॐ

Sometimes, Lord, I feel like I'm all alone in the world. Not that I ever consider myself superior to anyone else or more worthy. But it seems that a lot of people who claim to be Christians are saying and doing things that don't seem Christian at all! I'm not sure anymore who is truly a fellow seeker. And then I open Your Word and find that this has been happening for thousands of years, people not walking the walk or talking the talk. So help me not to be judgmental and not to compare myself with others but simply to continually seek You and experience Your way of peace so that I can live calmly within You. Amen.

Divine Implant

To everything there is a season, and a time for every matter or purpose under heaven. . . . A time to love and a time to hate, a time for war and a time for peace. . . . He also has planted eternity in men's hearts and minds [a divinely implanted sense of a purpose working through the ages which nothing under the sun but God alone can satisfy].

ECCLESIASTES 3:1, 8, 11 AMPC

In You, Lord, there's a time for everything, for every purpose—to live and die, plant and reap, kill and heal, break down and build up, weep and laugh, mourn and dance, get and lose, cast away and gather, rend and sew, keep silent and speak, love and hate, make war and make peace. Knowing these things will happen in my life and accepting those happenings as part and parcel of life helps me keep peace in perspective. But even more so does the fact that You've already planted within my heart and mind a sense of foreverness, a divine sense of purpose that only knowing, loving, and walking with You can satisfy. So help me remember that there will be times both good and bad—but all that really matters is my forever time with You. In Jesus' name, amen.

A Sense of Peace

May all go well with those who are right and good.
And may there be much peace until the moon is no
more. . . . For He will take out of trouble the one in
need when he cries for help, and the poor man who has
no one to help. He will have loving-pity on the weak
and those in need. He will save the lives of
those in need. He will take them from the
bad power that is held over them.
PSALM 72:7, 12–14 NLV

To know that someday justice will be served, that at
some point people will be helped and avenged, gives
me a sense of peace today. In the meantime, Lord,
help me do what I can to alleviate pain and increase
the right and good in the lives of people who have no
one to help. Use me as Your instrument to do what I
can for the helpless in the moment and leave what I
cannot do to You. Show me today where You would
have me help the helpless and give aid and offer prayers
for those who need them. In Jesus' name, amen.

Continually Unfolding the Past

I said, I will confess my transgressions to the Lord [continually unfolding the past till all is told]—then You [instantly] forgave me the guilt and iniquity. . . . For this [forgiveness] let everyone who is godly pray— pray to You in a time when You may be found; surely when the great waters [of trial] overflow, they shall not reach [the spirit in] him. You are a hiding place for me; You, Lord, preserve me from trouble.

PSALM 32:5–7 AMPC

My past is causing me some unrest, Lord. There are things I need to tell You, things I need to get off my chest, things You already know but that I have not yet confessed to You. So, Lord, here's some more of my backstory. . . .

Please, Lord, forgive me of all my missteps. And make good on Your promise to shield me from over-flowing waters of trials. Be my hiding place, my safe place, my sounding board as I continue to build my relationship with You. In Jesus' name, amen.

A Handful of Peaceful Repose

Luckier than the dead or the living is the person who has never even been, who has never seen the bad business that takes place on this earth. Then I observed all the work and ambition motivated by envy. What a waste! Smoke. And spitting into the wind. The fool sits back and takes it easy, his sloth is slow suicide. One handful of peaceful repose is better than two fistfuls of worried work.

ECCLESIASTES 4:3–6 MSG

Help me, Lord, not to take on too many of the trials and troubles of others, in addition to my own. Rein in my empathy or give me some other way to channel it so that instead of worrying I can do something constructive to help people who are having trouble or are troubled. And when it comes to work, Lord, help me not to fret over it but to lean back on it and have peace abound around it. Remind me to send up a prayer every step of the way so that my work will be seen as Your handiwork, signed, sealed, and delivered by Your Spirit. Amen.

Mind Life and Soul Peace

*Those who are according to the flesh and are controlled
by its unholy desires set their minds on and pursue
those things which gratify the flesh, but those who are
according to the Spirit and are controlled by the desires
of the Spirit set their minds on and seek those things
which gratify the [Holy] Spirit. Now the mind of the
flesh [which is sense and reason without the Holy
Spirit] is death. . . . But the mind of the
[Holy] Spirit is life and [soul] peace.*
ROMANS 8:5–6 AMPC

Too often, Lord, I find myself being controlled by un-
healthy desires, ones that have me looking to gratify
bodily yearnings above all else. But living that kind
of life gives me no sense of real peace at all. So I need
and want to change things up, to have my mind controlled by the desires of the Spirit. To set my mind on
seeking things that will please the Spirit. For then
and only then will I find peace for both my mind *and*
my soul. Amen.

Forever Peace

The people who walked in darkness have seen a great light; those who dwelt in a land of deep darkness, on them has light shone. . . . For to us a child is born, to us a son is given; and the government shall be upon his shoulder, and his name shall be called Wonderful Counselor, Mighty God, Everlasting Father, Prince of Peace. Of the increase of his government and of peace there will be no end.

ISAIAH 9:2, 6–7 ESV

There are some days more than others, Lord, when I desperately need to find my way back into Your light. So I come to You today for that extra bit of "Sonshine" I need to lift myself up out of the darkness of this world and pull free from the shadows that try to pull me down, out, and away from You. So here I am, Lord, opening myself up to Christ. Allow Him to fill me with His wisdom, strength, and eternal power, and most of all His forever peace, unlimited and unending. In Jesus' name I pray. Amen.

Power Down

People at the top. . .have it made. . .have nothing to worry about, not a care in the whole wide world. . . . Pretentious with arrogance, they wear the latest fashions in violence, pampered and overfed, decked out in silk bows of silliness. They jeer, using words to kill; they bully their way with words. They're full of hot air, loudmouths disturbing the peace. People actually listen to them—can you believe it? Like thirsty puppies, they lap up their words.
PSALM 73:3–4, 6–10 MSG

When I was younger, Lord, it seemed that people had more respect for one another and for the truth. But these days those things seem not to matter. And the only thing that does matter is money—who has it and who doesn't have it. But that's not going to matter in my life. I'm no longer going to worry about the "people at the top," those who seem to have it all. But I am going to ask You, Lord, to power down bullies in this town, county, state, and country. From all walks of life, all families, all jobs, and all people in government and beyond. Help me, Lord, to better discern peace breakers and spend more time with the peacemakers. In Jesus' name, amen.

Dos and Don'ts

Bless your enemies; no cursing under your breath.
Laugh with your happy friends when they're happy;
share tears when they're down. Get along with each
other; don't be stuck-up. Make friends with nobodies;
don't be the great somebody. Don't hit back; discover
beauty in everyone. If you've got it in you, get along
with everybody. Don't insist on getting even; that's not
for you to do. "I'll do the judging," says God.

ROMANS 12:14–19 MSG

Even though I myself am included in "people," Lord, I do not understand why people do what they do. Yet You would have me love them and live at peace with them whether I understand them or not. So please give me the strength to bless people who work against me. At the same time, give me the heart to laugh with my friends when they're happy and to cry with them when they're not. Show me the way to stay humble. And above all, Lord, help me to find something beautiful in every person I meet, to see the good within and not the bad. To look to make peace and live in love with all, in Jesus' name. Amen.

When All's Right

Right will build a home in the fertile field. And where there's Right, there'll be Peace and the progeny of Right: quiet lives and endless trust. My people will live in a peaceful neighborhood—in safe houses, in quiet gardens. The forest of your pride will be clear-cut, the city showing off your power leveled. But you will enjoy a blessed life, planting well-watered fields and gardens, with your farm animals grazing freely.

ISAIAH 32:16–20 MSG

There are days, Lord, when I despair of finding the peace I crave within and without. And then I enter the land of Your words, which soothe my soul and buoy my spirit. For You speak of how when all is right, we will find peace. And in that place of right and peace, I'll find the quiet life and endless trust I yearn for, surrounded by peace, safety, and calmness. Clear away my pride as if it were flammable brush. I know that I can only get to that place of peace with the help of Your words and Your powerful Spirit. Take me there now, Lord. Show me the freedom of a quiet life and endless trust. In Jesus' name, amen.

The Build Up

Let us no longer criticize one another. Instead decide never to put a stumbling block or pitfall in your brother's way. . . . The kingdom of God is not eating and drinking, but righteousness, peace, and joy in the Holy Spirit. Whoever serves Christ in this way is acceptable to God and approved by men. So then, we must pursue what promotes peace and what builds up one another.

ROMANS 14:13, 17–19 HCSB

I've seen the damage that divisive people can afflict on others, Lord. Even worse, there may have been times when I myself caused contention because I criticized someone. Whether my criticism was to make myself feel superior or to make another feel inferior doesn't seem to matter. For I know You would have me encourage rather than discourage the people in my life, whether they be strangers, relatives, friends, or enemies. So, in my effort to pursue peace and promote it, I'm determined to build others up and so bring Christ's light and love into their lives, allowing them to see and experience a bit of God's kingdom. For it is there that being right with God, the peace of Christ, and the joy of the Spirit reign. Amen.

Peace-Speak

I will listen to what God the Lord will say. For He will speak peace to His people, to those who are right with Him. But do not let them turn again to foolish things. For sure His saving power is near those who fear Him, so His shining-greatness may live in the land. Loving-kindness and truth have met together. Peace and what is right and good have kissed each other.

<small>PSALM 85:8–10 NLV</small>

Since You have entered my life, Jesus, things have been different. I'm seeing things more clearly, hearing and understanding what You would have me do or not do. But what I seem to be needing more and more of is a sense of peace. Lord, I want to live a life where no matter what is happening within me or around me, I'm still residing beside Your still waters and lying down in Your green pastures. So give me this moment, Lord, in which I can catch my breath as I lean back against You. After I willingly offer up my problems to You, Lord, speak Your peace to me. In Jesus' name, amen.

Hope and Harmony

Whatever was written in the past was written for
our instruction, so that we may have hope through
endurance and through the encouragement from the
Scriptures. Now may the God who gives endurance and
encouragement allow you to live in harmony with one
another, according to the command of Christ Jesus. . . .
Now may the God of hope fill you with all joy and peace
as you believe in Him so that you may overflow
with hope by the power of the Holy Spirit.

ROMANS 15:4–6, 13 HCSB

Your scriptures, Lord, are my gateway to You. Your
stories help me understand who You are and how I
can grow closer and closer to You. Your testaments encourage me to learn more about who You are and how
You see me. Your psalms read like my journal, where
a myriad of emotions and thoughts align so well with
my own. Your Word makes me feel loved, whole, and
full of hope. God of fortitude and confidence, help me
find a way to live in peace with others, just as Christ
commanded I do. Spirit of hope, fill me with Your joy
and peace. Amen.

Behind God's Back

This is the writing of Hezekiah king of Judah after he
had been sick and had recovered from his sickness. . . .
O give me back my health and make me live! Behold,
it was for my peace that I had intense bitterness;
but You have loved back my life from the pit of
corruption and nothingness, for You have
cast all my sins behind Your back.

ISAIAH 38:9, 16–17 AMPC

Sometimes, Lord, it's the bitterness of our lives that
leads us to seek You, to find You, to pray to You and
ask You things we would otherwise remain silent about.
Our needs, our desires, our predicaments draw us to
You time and time again. And time and time again,
during and after we pray to You, Lord, we find ourselves
overwhelmed by the power of Your peace and Your
love. For only You, Lord, could love us back away from
the edge of the cliff. Only You can grant the mercy
and forgiveness we need. Only You can be and are our
God. In Jesus' name, amen.

Rekindle

Stir up (rekindle the embers of, fan the flame of, and keep burning) the [gracious] gift of God, [the inner fire] that is in you. . . . For God did not give us a spirit of timidity (of cowardice, of craven and cringing and fawning fear), but [He has given us a spirit of] power and of love and of calm and well-balanced mind and discipline and self-control.

2 TIMOTHY 1:6–7 AMPC

Too often, Lord, I feel like I'm not living my life from a place of courage. I allow my fears to rule me more than my faith. Help me, Lord, to turn things around. Give me a new outlook. Help me rekindle my passion to use the gifts You've given me—and to do so without fear of the views or opinions of others. I serve and worship You alone. For You alone fuel me with a spirit of power, love, peace, clear thinking, discipline, and control, enabling me to do so much more than I ever asked or even imagined. In Jesus' name, amen.

Freed Up

*Walk and live [habitually] in the [Holy] Spirit
[responsive to and controlled and guided by the Spirit];
then you will certainly not gratify the cravings and
desires of the flesh (of human nature without God).
For the desires of the flesh are opposed to the [Holy]
Spirit, and the [desires of the] Spirit are opposed to
the flesh (godless human nature); for these
are antagonistic to each other [continually
withstanding and in conflict with each other].*

GALATIANS 5:16–17 AMPC

My Lord and Savior, Jesus, You have freed me up to
be exactly who our Father God created me to be: His
child. And yet sometimes I still find myself giving in
to the desires of my body. This ends up creating conflict, disrupting my peace within and without, because
the desires of my body are usually not at all the same
as the desires of the Spirit. So, help me, Lord, to be
more aware of what's controlling and guiding me. If
it's the Spirit, all's well. If the flesh, retrieve me from
my wandering. Pull me back toward You and Your
Spirit's way once more. Amen.

So Much

The Lord Who bought you and saves you, the Holy One of Israel, says, "I am the Lord your God, Who teaches you to do well, Who leads you in the way you should go. If only you had listened to My Laws! Then your peace would have been like a river and your right-standing with God would have been like the waves of the sea."

ISAIAH 48:17–18 NLV

Ah Lord, there is so much I owe You, so much You've done for me that I can never repay. Yet there are some things I *can* do to honor You. I can abide by Your teachings, so please make Your lessons plain, Lord. I can follow Your leading, so open my eyes to Your signposts. And I can listen to Your Word; open my ears so I can clearly hear You. Then I will have Your perpetual and constantly flowing peace. Then I will find Your blessings coming to me like waves rolling in from the sea. Ah Lord, there is so much I owe You, forever and ever. Amen.

From Distress to Peace

*In my distress I called to the LORD, and he answered
me. Deliver me, O LORD, from lying lips, from a
deceitful tongue. . . . Woe to me, that I sojourn in
Meshech, that I dwell among the tents of Kedar!
Too long have I had my dwelling among those
who hate peace. I am for peace, but when
I speak, they are for war!*
PSALM 120:1–2, 5–7 ESV

My heart aches and longs for people who know and
will speak the truth, Lord. For I don't know who to
believe anymore, except for You. So, Lord, when I
cry out, be quick to turn Your ear to me, to listen, to
deliver me. Separate me, Lord, from those who lie
to gain, manipulate, retain the status quo, whatever.
Bring people into my life who are truthful and humble.
People who dislike conflict as much as I do. And give
me the right words to say so that I can calm people
down and practice peace myself. Help me, Lord, to
change my conversation so that when people hear
my words, they will recognize I am for peace. Amen.

In Good Hands

The fruit of the [Holy] Spirit [the work which His presence within accomplishes] is love, joy (gladness), peace, patience (an even temper, forbearance), kindness, goodness (benevolence), faithfulness, gentleness (meekness, humility), self-control (self-restraint, continence). . . . If we live by the [Holy] Spirit, let us also walk by the Spirit. [If by the Holy Spirit we have our life in God, let us go forward walking in line, our conduct controlled by the Spirit.]

GALATIANS 5:22–23, 25 AMPC

❧

Lord, You have created me, Your Son has saved me, and Your Spirit produces in me all the positive characteristics—love, joy, peace, patience, kindness, goodness, faithfulness, gentleness, self-control—of a godly daughter. Help me, Lord, to allow Your Spirit to work in me in every and any way He can. Make me look, speak, act, listen, and walk just as Jesus did. I wish to follow in His steps, even though at times I know that road may be rocky. Still, no matter what the terrain, I know I am in good hands, moving forward, my steps solidly in line with Yours and my actions controlled by Your Spirit. Amen.

The News

*"Seek the LORD while he may be found; call upon
him while he is near; let the wicked forsake his way,
and the unrighteous man his thoughts; let him return to
the LORD. . . . For my thoughts are not your thoughts,
neither are your ways my ways, declares the LORD.
For as the heavens are higher than the earth,
so are my ways higher than your ways
and my thoughts than your thoughts."*

ISAIAH 55:6–9 ESV

Lord, although I don't consider myself very wicked
or unrighteous, I am having a difficult time with my
mind-set. I feel I'm being inundated with nothing but
bad news. And that bad news affects my thoughts,
leading me to despair, conflict, and hopelessness. So
here I am, Lord, coming to You once more for some
much-needed help. Give me the strength to memorize
Your Word (a.k.a. thoughts) so that I can live my
life more in line with how You would have me live
it. Help me spend less time watching, reading, and
listening to the world news and more time watching,
reading, and listening to Your Good News. In Jesus'
name, amen.

The Real Thing

While there has never been any question about your
honesty in these matters—I couldn't be more proud of
you!—I want you also to be smart, making sure every
"good" thing is the real thing. Don't be gullible in regard
to smooth-talking evil. Stay alert like this, and before
you know it the God of peace will come down on
Satan with both feet, stomping him into
the dirt. Enjoy the best of Jesus!
ROMANS 16:19–20 MSG

There are times, Lord, when I feel so gullible, so naive.
Too many times I am fooled, tricked, taken in. So
here I am before You, asking You to give me wisdom
to see beyond facades. Reveal to me what is real and
what is not. And keep me alert to the wiles of others
so that I can tell the difference between the godly and
ungodly. In the meantime, I thank You, my God of
peace, for watching over me, protecting me, keeping
me close and in Your care, and loving me. In Jesus'
name I pray. Amen.

The Power of the Word

*"The rain and snow come down from heaven and do
not return there without giving water to the earth.
This makes plants grow on the earth, and gives seeds
to the planter and bread to the eater. So My Word
which goes from My mouth will not return to Me
empty. It will do what I want it to do, and will
carry out My plan well. You will go out
with joy, and be led out in peace."*

ISAIAH 55:10–12 NLV

So much power resides within Your Word, Lord.
Whatever You say, whatever flows from Your mouth,
in no way returns to You empty. For Your Word does
whatever You want it to do. It carries out Your plans,
ideas, purpose. The beauty and wonder of it is that Your
Word holds so much power for and within me—and
it is there for me to tap into anytime day or night. So,
Lord, today, along with Your blessing me with Your
strength, bless me with Your peace as I live within and
by Your Word. In Jesus' name I pray. Amen.

The Important Thing

I do not want to be proud of anything except in the cross of our Lord Jesus Christ. Because of the cross, the ways of this world are dead to me, and I am dead to them. If a person does or does not go through the religious act of becoming a Jew, it is worth nothing. The important thing is to become a new person. Those who follow this way will have God's peace and loving-kindness. They are the people of God.

GALATIANS 6:14–16 NLV

You have begun a new work in me, Lord. You, Your Son, and Your Spirit, as well as Your Word, have begun to transform me, to make me into a new woman, a woman of God. To get there from here, Lord, I need Your supernatural power and support, as well as some new strength every day. I need Your help as I learn to live and move in Your Spirit, to refresh, renew, and transform my mind, to sing this new song You have composed and planted in my heart. And I thank You for giving me Your peace and loving-kindness as I follow this way. In Jesus' name, amen.

Peace like a River

*For thus says the Lord: Behold, I will extend peace
to her like a river, and the glory of the nations like an
overflowing stream; then you will be nursed, you will be
carried on her hip and trotted [lovingly bounced up and
down] on her [God's maternal] knees. As one whom
his mother comforts, so will I comfort you;
you shall be comforted in Jerusalem.*

ISAIAH 66:12–13 AMPC

Oh Lord, what I wouldn't do to have peace like a
river attending my way, helping me live a life for You
in such a chaotic world during such a chaotic time.
Yet peace is not just what You promised me but also
what You left me (John 14:27). You don't just give
me peace; You care for me as a mother cares for her
darling child. You nourish me, Abba, as no one else
can. You allow me to cling to You as You carry me on
Your hip. You even lovingly bounce me up and down
on Your knee. Remind me of this promised peace and
Your attention to care, Lord, when anxiety comes to
call. Continue to comfort me as no one else but You
can. In Jesus' name, amen.

Peace Talk

*A meal of bread and water in contented peace is better
than a banquet spiced with quarrels. . . . Evil people
relish malicious conversation; the ears of liars itch
for dirty gossip. . . . A quiet rebuke to a person of
good sense does more than a whack on the head of
a fool. . . . The start of a quarrel is like a leak
in a dam, so stop it before it bursts.*

PROVERBS 17:1, 4, 10, 14 MSG

❧

Words, written and spoken, hold so much power, Lord.
They can hurt or heal, break down or build up, anger
or comfort, criticize or compliment. As a follower of
You, Lord, I ask for Your help to use my words to lift
people up, not bring them down—to encourage, not
discourage; to praise, not complain; to love, not hate;
to help, not hinder. Make me more aware of my words,
Lord, *before they leave my mouth!* Help me be a woman
who talks peace, bringing people together rather than
tearing them apart. And may these words I speak—to
myself and others—be ones that would draw all closer
to You. Amen.

God Calling

God has called us to peace. For, wife, how can you be
sure of converting and saving your husband? Husband,
how can you be sure of converting and saving your
wife? Only, let each one [seek to conduct himself and
regulate his affairs so as to] lead the life which the
Lord has allotted and imparted to him and to
which God has invited and summoned him.

1 Corinthians 7:15–17 AMPC

You have called me to a life of peace, Lord. But I need
Your help. For that life of peace can be challenged by
marriage. How I behave can draw my partner either
toward You or away from You. So I'm going to need
not only Your unlimited strength but Your wisdom.
Lord, help me be a good example of a Christ follower.
Help me lead the life You created me to lead, a life
rich with peace, love, joy, understanding, and hope.
Make me a woman who not only keeps her husband
interested in her but leads him closer and closer to You.
Abba God, Lord Jesus, and Holy Spirit, be with me
as I answer Your call to peace. In Jesus' name, amen.

My Maker

*Fear not, for you shall not be ashamed; neither be
confounded and depressed, for you shall not be put to
shame. For you shall forget the shame of your youth,
and you shall not [seriously] remember the reproach of
your widowhood any more. For your Maker is your
Husband—the Lord of hosts is His name—and the
Holy One of Israel is your Redeemer; the God
of the whole earth He is called.*

ISAIAH 54:4–5 AMPC

Life can be lonely, Lord, whether a person is married,
single, or widowed. That's why I take such joy in
looking to You to fulfill me in every way. For You have
claimed that You, my Maker, are also my Husband. You,
the Lord of Hosts, are my Redeemer. You, the God of
the whole earth, are also my Father, my Beloved, my
Rock and Refuge. Knowing You are all things to me,
from A to Z, I will not fear nor be ashamed, confused,
or depressed. Because You are my all in all, there is
nothing else and no one else I need to feel complete,
loved, and chosen. Thank You, my Savior, for loving
me so. In Jesus' name, amen.

Mother Wisdom

Wisdom cries aloud in the street, she raises her voice in the markets. . . . If you will turn (repent) and give heed to my reproof, behold, I [Wisdom] will pour out my spirit upon you, I will make my words known to you. . . . Whoso hearkens to me [Wisdom] shall dwell securely and in confident trust and shall be quiet, without fear or dread of evil.

PROVERBS 1:20, 23, 33 AMPC

Oh God of wisdom, I seek Your help and advice. Please answer my call. Pour out Your Spirit on me. Then, as You speak to my mind and heart, help me comprehend Your words. Answer my questions, make clear Your response, and give me tools to apply Your knowledge and understanding to my life. Help me not to be too sensitive when You scold me but to take Your advice and allow it to draw me ever closer to You. I ask all these things knowing that the more I heed Your wisdom, the securer I'll be and the more I'll live in peace, with trust, confidence, and courage. Amen.

A Forever Kind of Love

"This exile is just like the days of Noah for me:
I promised then that the waters of Noah would never
again flood the earth. I'm promising now no more anger,
no more dressing you down. For even if the mountains
walk away and the hills fall to pieces, my love won't
walk away from you, my covenant commitment
of peace won't fall apart." The GOD who
has compassion on you says so.

ISAIAH 54:9–10 MSG

How soothing, how wonderful, how lovely to know, Lord, that You have promised me a forever kind of love. Even if mountains are leveled and hills fall into the sea, You will continue to love me. No matter what happens, Your covenant of peace will neither be shaken nor fall apart. Your love for me, for all Your daughters, is more than I can take in, Lord. There are very few things in my life that are certain, and You, Lord, are one of them. Thank You for loving me through the rough patches, for sticking with me when all others deserted me. My love won't walk away from You. Amen.

Cool and Calm

He [Who is the source of their prophesying] is not a God
of confusion and disorder but of peace and order. . . .
So [to conclude], my brethren, earnestly desire and set
your hearts on prophesying (on being inspired to preach
and teach and to interpret God's will and purpose), and
do not forbid or hinder speaking in [unknown] tongues.
But all things should be done. . .in an orderly fashion.

1 CORINTHIANS 14:33, 39–40 AMPC

Lord, my life is, at times, full of confusion. Sometimes
my church is as well. But that's not what You would
want me or Your church to be. So when I find myself
feeling unsettled, Lord, help me to take that as a sign
that I need to stop in my tracks, come to You, and pray
for Your peace and order to fill me. And, when I'm at
church, Lord, feeling like I've just landed in a panic
room, prompt me to pray for my fellow believers, that
You would lift the spirit of confusion and disorder and
rain down Your peace and order. May my praying in and
saying Jesus' name fill me with Your cool-headedness
and calmness. Amen.

Praying for Peace

*All your [spiritual] children shall be disciples [taught by
the Lord and obedient to His will], and great shall
be the peace and undisturbed composure of your
children. You shall establish yourself in righteousness
(rightness, in conformity with God's will and order):
you shall be far from even the thought of oppression
or destruction, for you shall not fear, and from
terror, for it shall not come near you.*

ISAIAH 54:13–14 AMPC

❧

I long, Lord, for peace of mind, heart, body, soul, and
spirit. And that's just what You promise, not only
for me but for the children of the future. So, Lord,
today I pray that You would keep me far from danger.
That You would remove from my mind any thoughts
of destruction. Extract from my heart any bitterness
that may darken its corridors. Silence my lips around
disparaging remarks. Keep my hands from working
plans away from You and my feet from walking roads
away from You. And most of all, Lord, keep fear a far
distance from me and courage intimately close. In
Jesus' name I pray for such peace. Amen.

Loving

Jesus said to him, "'You must love the Lord your
God with all your heart and with all your soul and
with all your mind.' This is the first and greatest
of the Laws. The second is like it, 'You must love
your neighbor as you love yourself.' All the
Laws and the writings of the early preachers
depend on these two most important Laws."

MATTHEW 22:37–40 NLV

Today, Lord, I pray for the people of the world to heed
Jesus' greatest commandments. To love You with all
their heart, soul, and mind, and to love their neigh-
bors as they love themselves. For, Lord, if everyone
in the world loved You above all things and others as
well as themselves, there would be no wars or crimes.
People would be looking out for each other, helping
each other, taking care of each other—and loving
You. Along with praying for others to love, I ask You,
Lord, to help me to love others—beginning with You.
To do so gladly and with my entire being. Help me to
love myself, which can be difficult at times, so that I
can learn how to love others. In Jesus' name, amen.

The Ideal Servant

*Whoever stirs up strife against you shall fall and
surrender to you. . . . But no weapon that is formed
against you shall prosper, and every tongue that shall
rise against you in judgment you shall show to be in
the wrong. This [peace, righteousness, security,
triumph over opposition] is the heritage of the
servants of the Lord [those in whom the
ideal Servant of the Lord is reproduced].*

ISAIAH 54:15, 17 AMPC

❧

Oh Lord, I love the idea that anyone who comes up
against me will end up surrendering to me. Even better,
that no weapon fashioned against me will succeed,
whether that weapon be a sword of metal or a tongue
of flesh. No matter how powerful anything is or looks,
no matter how much money a person wields, You,
Lord, promise to protect and defend me. Yet there's a
caveat. This protection, this great peace and security,
is available only to God followers who resemble Jesus
Christ, people in whom He is replicated. Help me
become that girl of God, a woman who is a copy of the
God-man who saved us all. In His name I pray. Amen.

Blindingly Obvious

Be cheerful. Keep things in good repair. Keep your spirits up. Think in harmony. Be agreeable. Do all that, and the God of love and peace will be with you for sure. Greet one another with a holy embrace. All the brothers and sisters here say hello. The amazing grace of the Master, Jesus Christ, the extravagant love of God, the intimate friendship of the Holy Spirit, be with all of you.

2 CORINTHIANS 13:11–14 MSG

Lord, I want to do what You would have me do, to follow Your lead in all things. Yet oftentimes I am going to need Your help, for some things don't come to me as naturally as they do for others. So, as I walk this road with You, Lord, help me to have an optimistic outlook. To see and focus on the good in all things and people, even if the not so good is blindingly obvious. Help me encourage others, including myself, by planting good words and seeds of love in their midst. Give me a mind that thinks with compassion, not conflict. And as I do these things, Lord, may it be blindingly obvious to others that You, the God of peace and love, are with me. Amen.

Within Your Walls

I was glad when they said to me, "Let us go to the house of the Lord." . . . May all go well for those who love you. May there be peace within your walls. May all go well within your houses. I will now say, "May peace be within you," for the good of my brothers and my friends. Because of the house of the Lord our God, I will pray for your good.

PSALM 122:1, 6–9 NLV

Something happens to me, Lord, when I come into Your house, when I step into Your sanctuary, Your place of peace. That's when I am most conscious of Your world totally surrounding me—my walls within Yours and Your walls within mine. Me in You and You in me is a safe place to be in a world often fraught with conflict. Help me, Lord, to carry that sense of place and peace within myself so that wherever I am my connection to You is firm and sure. And as I appropriate Your peace, Lord, and make it my own, give me the opportunity to share it with others. To bless them with peace within their walls, houses, and deep within. May Your peace reign. Amen.

Undisturbed

*May grace (God's unmerited favor) and spiritual peace
[which means peace with God and harmony, unity,
and undisturbedness] be yours from God our Father and
from the Lord Jesus Christ. . . . You who once were [so]
far away, through (by, in) the blood of Christ have been
brought near. For He is [Himself] our peace
(our bond of unity and harmony).*

Ephesians 1:2; 2:13–14 AMPC

Grace, favor, peace, harmony, unity, undisturbedness,
brought near—the beauty of these words, Lord, leaves
me breathless. In these days, these words seem rarely
used, for they are not reflective of the atmosphere in
which we now live. And that is why I seek You, why I
love delving into Your Word, why I continually plant
Your Good News within my heart. Today, Lord, pour
down upon me, refresh me with, Your grace and peace.
Draw me ever closer so that I may feel Your presence
and take in Your energy, life, and light. You—God,
Jesus, Spirit—are my peace, my path, my passion, my
provision. Keep me by Your side, undisturbed by the
woes of the world, knowing You alone *are* my world.
In Jesus' name I pray. Amen.

Silence before God

" 'I'll be right there with [Jerusalem]'—GOD's Decree—
'a wall of fire around unwalled Jerusalem and a
radiant presence within.' " . . . Quiet, everyone!
Shh! Silence before GOD. Something's afoot in his
holy house. He's on the move! . . . . When the Lamb
ripped off the seventh seal, Heaven fell quiet—
complete silence for about half an hour.

ZECHARIAH 2:4–5, 13; REVELATION 8:1 MSG

ॐ

In this ever-restless world, Lord, finding a place of quiet
is difficult. People are more apt to talk than listen,
Lord. Or else they escape the world's silence by filling
their emptiness with mindless games, social media,
texts, emails, and the like. It's all still noise, all still a
distraction. Yet my path to You, Lord, is paved with
silence. For it's only when I truly empty my mind and
heart of all but You that I find my place before You,
beside You, sharing my thoughts, dreams, ideas—and
life. Thank You, Lord, for taking the time to sit still
with me, to rest, to find true and holy peace of mind,
heart, spirit, and soul. Come, greet me, Lord, as I enter
into Your silence, Your presence, Your love. Amen.

From the Heart

I ask you from my heart to live and work the way the Lord expected you to live and work. Live and work without pride. Be gentle and kind. Do not be hard on others. Let love keep you from doing that. Work hard to live together as one by the help of the Holy Spirit. Then there will be peace.

EPHESIANS 4:1–3 NLV

Lord, I'm looking not just for peace within, although that's where it begins, but for peace without. For peace between me and the next man or woman. So, Lord, please show me; lead me to what You want me to do, how You want me to live. Fill my head, hands, and heart with the inspiration I need to do what You've called me to do, to work as You've called me to work, to live as You would have me live. Put pride far from me and bring gentleness and kindness in close. Help me to treat others with compassion and love, just like I'd want to be treated. And above all, Lord, give myself and my fellow believers the aid and unity of Your Holy Spirit so we can live as one, in One, for One, in peace. In Jesus' name I pray. Amen.

In the Unseen

*You have seen my affliction, You have taken note of my
life's distresses, and. . .You have set my feet in a broad
place. . . . Oh, how great is Your goodness, which You
have laid up for those who fear, revere, and worship
You, goodness which You have wrought for those who
trust and take refuge in You before the sons of men!
In the secret place of Your presence You hide them.*
PSALM 31:7–8, 19–20 AMPC

When I'm tired, when I'm fraught with worries, when
I'm desperate for some peace and one-on-one time
with You, I find my way to that secret place I share
with You alone. You, Lord, have seen the challenges
I face, the opportunities they bring. You alone know
everything I've ever done, thought, and said. You
know me inside and out—and still You love me. Still
You rescue me, giving me the guidance and direction
I need to find my way. So here I am once more, Lord,
coming to You, finding You in that special secret place
in the unseen where peace, love, light, and You are
found. Ah, that's better. Amen.

The Search

I know the thoughts and plans that I have for you,
says the Lord, thoughts and plans for welfare and peace
and not for evil, to give you hope in your final outcome.
Then you will call upon Me, and you will come and
pray to Me, and I will hear and heed you. Then you
will seek Me, inquire for, and require Me [as a
vital necessity] and find Me when you
search for Me with all your heart.
JEREMIAH 29:11–13 AMPC

Lord, I know You have plans for me. Yet I feel I'm not where I thought I'd be at this point in my life. I expected something different, perhaps something better. And I'm a bit concerned over what lies ahead. So help me, Lord, to trust You with my future. For I know You have thought and planned for me since before I was a twinkle in my father's eye or a smile on my mother's lips. You have prepared a good outcome for me, for peace in my life and not evil, all so that I will have hope in my future. Open my ears to Your Word, open my soul to Your love, open my spirit to Your peace as I search for You with all of my heart. Amen.

Standing Strong

Take all the help you can get, every weapon God has issued, so that when it's all over but the shouting you'll still be on your feet. Truth, righteousness, peace, faith, and salvation are more than words. Learn how to apply them. You'll need them throughout your life. God's Word is an indispensable weapon. In the same way, prayer is essential in this ongoing warfare. Pray hard and long.

EPHESIANS 6:13–18 MSG

❧

I live in a topsy-turvy world, Lord. And I need all the help I can get. That's where You come in. Give me all the tools I need to be able to stand strong when challenges come my way. For with Your help, those challenges can be turned into opportunities for You to work through me in the world. Teach me, Lord, how to apply truth, right standing, peace, faith, and salvation to my life. Help me plant Your Word in my heart so that I'll have its support when the going gets tough. And most of all, Lord, help me then go deeper with prayer, the next greatest weapon available. What a comfort knowing You have provided me with all I need to be the woman You created me to be in this world and the next. Amen.

Round About

Those who trust in, lean on, and confidently hope in the Lord are like Mount Zion, which cannot be moved but abides and stands fast forever. As the mountains are round about Jerusalem, so the Lord is round about His people from this time forth and forever. . . . Do good, O Lord, to those who are good, and to those who are right [with You and all people] in their hearts.

PSALM 125:1–2, 4 AMPC

When I'm unsettled, frightened, unsure, stressed, worried, and overwhelmed, I run to You, Lord. For You are the one person, the one Spirit, the one God above all gods I trust. Others lean on humans. But humans are fallible. That's why I lean on You and hope in You alone. You, like Mount Zion, cannot be moved. You will be and always have been there for me, holding me, helping me. Like the mountains that surround and protect Jerusalem, You surround and protect me. And You've promised to do so forever and ever. So as I come to You today, Lord, as I lean into Your loving arms, surround me with Your love, protection, and peace. Shield me from this foreign land until I arrive back home with You. Amen.

Calling to God

*Call to Me and I will answer you and show you great
and mighty things, fenced in and hidden, which you
do not know (do not distinguish and recognize,
have knowledge of and understand). . . . [In the
future restored Jerusalem] I will lay upon it health
and healing, and I will cure them and will reveal
to them the abundance of peace (prosperity,
security, stability) and truth.*

JEREMIAH 33:3, 6 AMPC

Some days, Lord, I run around behaving more like a
chicken with her head cut off than a daughter of the
God above all gods. And this seems to be one of those
"fowl" days. So, Lord, I'm calling on You, asking You
to hear my prayer, heed my words. Show me, Lord,
what I need to know, those "great and mighty things"
I may not understand. Reveal the things that have
been hidden from my earthly eyes. Open up Your
storehouse of knowledge so that I can understand or
recognize the work You are doing in my life and in
my world. For You are the source of restoration. You
are my pathway to health and healing, to peace and
prosperity, to trust and truth. Lord, please, answer my
call. Rain down Your peace. Amen.

The Power of Peace

*To all these things, you must add love. Love holds
everybody and everything together. . . . Let the peace of
Christ have power over your hearts. You were chosen
as a part of His body. Always be thankful. Let the
teaching of Christ and His words keep on living in you.
These make your lives rich and full of wisdom. Keep on
teaching and helping each other. Sing. . .the songs
of heaven with hearts full of thanks to God.*

COLOSSIANS 3:14–16 NLV

I feel like I'm in a battle, Lord. Within and without, my
peace has taken flight. And so to You I come, looking
to You for help and for Your love, which holds all
things together, because You Yourself are love. Also,
Lord, I come looking for peace. Help me surrender
myself to You, to let You have full sway over my entire
being—mind, body, heart, soul, and spirit—so that the
peace of Christ can have full rein in my heart. And as
I bow down before You, Lord, plant Your Word within
me. Teach me what You would have me know, what
You would have me say, what You would have me do
to help others. Amen.

Blessed Quiet for Your Soul

*Come to Me, all you who labor and are heavy-laden
and overburdened, and I will cause you to rest. [I will
ease and relieve and refresh your souls.] Take My yoke
upon you and learn of Me, for I am gentle (meek)
and humble (lowly) in heart, and you will find rest
(relief and ease and refreshment and recreation
and blessed quiet) for your souls.*

MATTHEW 11:28–29 AMPC

❧

Lord, I come to You in this moment, my back aching
from the load I've been carrying. It's too much for me
to bear. So I leave it at Your feet. Please, Jesus, give
me the relief I so desperately need. Help me recover
my life, my heart, my soul from the pressures of this
world. Lead me to Your kingdom so that I can find
the relief and ease I need. Show me, Lord, how to
take a real break, a real rest. Help me get back into
Your rhythm, to walk in step with You, to take a deep
breath and relax, and to allow You to replace my
problems with Your peace. Bless my soul, Jesus, with
Your quiet. Amen.

The Link to All Good

Praise the Lord, O my soul. And all that is within me,
praise His holy name. Praise the Lord, O my soul.
And forget none of His acts of kindness. He forgives
all my sins. He heals all my diseases. He saves my life
from the grave. He crowns me with loving-kindness
and pity. He fills my years with good things and
I am made young again like the eagle.

PSALM 103:1–5 NLV

When panic or problems threaten to steal my joy and peace in You, Lord, You bring to mind all the things for which I can praise You. And as I begin to think back to how much You've done for me and with me, as my mind fills with all the blessings—past and present, earthly and heavenly—I have in You, my panic melts away and my problems dissipate. So, I thank You, Lord, for Your kindness, forgiveness, healing power, and compassion. Thank You for filling my years here on this earth with so many good things. But most of all, thank You, Lord, for being my link to all that is good, loving, peaceful, and eternal. Amen.

Looking Up

If then you have been raised with Christ [to a new life, thus sharing His resurrection from the dead], aim at and seek the [rich, eternal treasures] that are above, where Christ is, seated at the right hand of God. And set your minds and keep them set on what is above (the higher things), not on the things that are on the earth. For [as far as this world is concerned] you have died, and your [new, real] life is hidden with Christ in God.

COLOSSIANS 3:1–3 AMPC

❧

I'm losing my peace, Lord, and I think it's because my eyes are in the wrong place. It seems I've been focusing on everything *except* for You. So help me raise my sights, Lord. Lift my head so I can seek the things that are above this earth, the forever riches I have in knowing You and Your Son. Lift my eyes and mind, Lord, so that I may see the higher things, such as peace, love, understanding, compassion, empathy, and wisdom. Each day, lift my thoughts, Lord, ever higher. Transform my mind, shape my thoughts, so that each day I may become more like Jesus, my Hero, Savior, and Prince of Peace. In His name I pray. Amen.

Turn Things Around

*"I will turn things around for the people. I'll give them a
language undistorted, unpolluted, words to address God
in worship and, united, to serve me with their shoulders
to the wheel. . . . I'll leave a core of people among you
who are poor in spirit. . . . They'll make their home
in God. This core holy people will not do wrong. . . .
Content with who they are and where they
are, unanxious, they'll live at peace."*
ZEPHANIAH 3:9, 12–13 MSG

Lord, what peace I would have within myself if I could
just be content with who I am and where I am. I keep
comparing myself to other people, people who seem to
have a better life. Yet those same people are as tran-
sient as I am. You have said, Lord, that Your people
are foreigners here. We are strangers on this earth, for
this is not our true home. So help me, Lord, to take
my eyes off myself and focus them on You. Show me
ways to make my home in You, content to be who You
made me and to be where You have placed me. Free,
easy, and at peace in You. Amen.

By Heart

*Do not forget my teaching. Let your heart keep
my words. For they will add to you many days and
years of life and peace. Do not let kindness and truth
leave you. Tie them around your neck. Write them
upon your heart. So you will find favor and good
understanding in the eyes of God and man.*

PROVERBS 3:1–4 NLV

When I'm confused and unsettled, Lord, lead me into
Your Word. Show me what You would have me know.
And when I've understood, when I've applied Your
Word to my life, help me not just to take Your teaching
to heart but to learn it by heart. For I have discovered
the power of Your Word. When I recall Your verses that
I've stored in my mind, they wield so much force and
emit so much strength within and without that I can't
help but find myself amazed. And once the amazement
fades, I'm left with joy and peace—joy that You have
once more rescued me and peace that You have once
more been there for me. Today, Lord, continue my
education. Lead me to Your next teaching and the
next words to write on my heart. Amen.

Vibrant Harmonies

*From beginning to end he's there, towering far above
everything, everyone. So spacious is he, so roomy,
that everything of God finds its proper place in him
without crowding. Not only that, but all the broken and
dislocated pieces of the universe—people and things,
animals and atoms—get properly fixed and fit together
in vibrant harmonies, all because of his death,
his blood that poured down from the cross.*

Colossians 1:18–20 msg

Jesus, my Lord and Savior, when I think of all You went through to save someone like me, I am very humbled and grateful. For it was through Your innocent blood shed on the cross that our Father made His peace with us. All the broken bits, all the loose ends, all the creatures and creations in the universe were made whole and complete once more through You. Because of You, everything has now been repaired, remade, renewed, and refreshed. All is in harmony because of Your death. Yet because You still live, because I still have access to You, I also have access to Your peace. Help me, Lord, to live a life in tune with You. Amen.

Battle Positions

The Lord says this to you: Be not afraid or dismayed at this great multitude; for the battle is not yours, but God's. . . . You shall not need to fight in this battle; take your positions, stand still, and see the deliverance of the Lord [Who is] with you. . . . Fear not nor be dismayed. Tomorrow go out against them, for the Lord is with you.

2 CHRONICLES 20:15, 17 AMPC

Lately, Lord, every time I turn around I feel as if I'm in another war, fighting some other kind of battle in addition to the ones I'm already in the midst of. This is exhausting. It's no way to live. I need some peace in my life, Lord. So here I am before You, asking You, Lord, to help me. Give me the wisdom to discern what battles You would have me fight and which You would have me just stand back and watch You fight. Both options take a lot of faith, trust, and courage, a few more of the things I need. So there it is, Lord. Show me the position You would have me take as I stand with You in faith. Amen.

Plain and Straight

*Lean on, trust in, and be confident in the Lord with
all your heart and mind and do not rely on your own
insight or understanding. In all your ways know,
recognize, and acknowledge Him, and He will direct
and make straight and plain your paths. Be not wise in
your own eyes; reverently fear and worship the Lord
and turn [entirely] away from evil.*

PROVERBS 3:5–7 AMPC

I remember as a child how much I hated not having control over my life, Lord. Grown-ups were always telling me where to go and what to do. Yet now that I *am* a grown-up, part of me would, at times, like *not* to have to be the decision maker, because more often than not I have no idea where to go and what to do, or how or when to do it. I'm too afraid of making the wrong choice. Thus, instead of doing something, anything, I do nothing. So, Lord, for my peace of mind and heart, I turn all my questions over to You. In Your wisdom, Lord, show me the path You would have me take as You make my path plain and straight. Amen.

The Head-Lifting God

We couldn't settle down. The fights in the church and
the fears in our hearts kept us on pins and needles.
We couldn't relax because we didn't know how it would
turn out. Then the God who lifts up the downcast lifted
our heads and our hearts with the arrival of Titus.
We were glad just to see him, but the true reassurance
came in. . .how much you cared, how much
you grieved, how concerned you were for me.
I went from worry to tranquility in no time!

2 CORINTHIANS 7:5–7 MSG

᪥

So often battles are going on outside me while at
the same time I'm fending off fears within me, Lord.
Being so conflicted within and without makes it hard
to be able to relax. And constantly worrying about
how things will turn out in the end doesn't do much
for my peace of mind and heart. But then You send
someone or something my way—an encourager or a
blessing—and suddenly I'm looking up once more. I'm
remembering how much You care for me. And before
I know it, frets fly out the window and peace stills my
soul. Thank You, Lord, for being the Lifter of my head
and my heart. Amen.

Sweet Sleep

*Keep sound and godly Wisdom and discretion, and they
will be life to your inner self, and a gracious ornament
to your neck (your outer self). Then you will walk in
your way securely and in confident trust, and you shall
not dash your foot or stumble. When you lie down,
you shall not be afraid; yes, you shall lie down,
and your sleep shall be sweet.*

PROVERBS 3:21–24 AMPC

My day usually begins well, Lord, because I wake up
with You in my mind and heart. But then, as my day
goes on, I get distracted with the world. Before I know
it, I'm doing, working, living, loving in my wisdom and
strength, not Yours. That's when things start to fall
apart. That's when I start to trip over my own thoughts
and end up flat on my face. By the end of the day, I'm
beaten and bruised and sleep becomes elusive at best.
So help me regain my peace by keeping and following
Your wisdom and ways all through my day. As I do, I
know I'll find calm and sweet sleep in the secret place
of Your presence. In Jesus' name, amen.

Right Place for Peace

Break off your sins and show the reality of your repentance by righteousness (right standing with God and moral and spiritual rectitude and rightness in every area and relation) and liberate yourself from your iniquities by showing mercy and loving-kindness to the poor and oppressed, that [if the king will repent] there may possibly be a continuance and lengthening of your peace and tranquility and a healing of your error.

DANIEL 4:27 AMPC

Sometimes, Lord, to get some peace in life, it's up to me to get myself in the right place spiritually. I need to take the time to look at my life, my walk, and my talk and get myself realigned with You. So show me, Lord, where I am being misled in my walk with You. What should I stop doing and what should I start doing? Point out my missteps and misdirection, Lord, so that I can get back on the right path to You and the peace I crave—and perhaps even find a way to repair whatever mistakes I've made. In Jesus' name, amen.

Sit Back and Relax

*Ruth told her everything that the man had done for her,
adding, "And he gave me all this barley besides—six
quarts! He told me, 'You can't go back empty-handed to
your mother-in-law!'" Naomi said, "Sit back and relax,
my dear daughter, until we find out how things turn out;
that man isn't going to fool around. Mark my words,
he's going to get everything wrapped up today."*
RUTH 3:16–18 MSG

When I'm waiting to see how things are going to turn
out, Lord, I don't just get anxious; I also get grouchy.
Then before I know it, all kinds of scenarios begin
playing out in my mind. And soon, any semblance of
peace that remained within me has taken flight. So
help me take the advice that Naomi gave to Ruth,
Lord. Help me not to worry or freak out over imaginary
scenarios that may never come to pass, and instead
"sit back and relax" until I see how things are going to
turn out. Help me to leave all in Your hands, knowing
You always know best. In Jesus' name, amen.

Right with God

"Do not worry. Do not keep saying, 'What will we eat?'
or, 'What will we drink?' or, 'What will we wear?'
The people who do not know God are looking for all
these things. Your Father in heaven knows you need
all these things. First of all, look for the holy nation
of God. Be right with Him. All these other
things will be given to you also."

MATTHEW 6:31–33 NLV

❧

One of my major challenges in life, Lord, is not worrying about anything and everything but leaving all my concerns and questions in Your hands. For that's the only way I'll be able to maintain the amazing peace I found in You when I first believed. Help me to remember that You, Lord, know everything I need in this world and beyond. In fact, You know—and have already waiting in the wings—all those things I'm going to need before they've even entered into my head. So, Lord, from now on, to maintain my peace, my first priority is to be right with You. My second is to trust that whatever I do need is already on its way. Amen.

Your Confidence

Be not afraid of sudden terror and panic, nor of the stormy blast or the storm and ruin of the wicked when it comes [for you will be guiltless], for the Lord shall be your confidence, firm and strong, and shall keep your foot from being caught [in a trap or some hidden danger].

PROVERBS 3:25–26 AMPC

There's no peace for me, Lord, when I allow my imagination to run wild. When I hear of a danger, something bad that may or may not happen, the next thing I know, my mind is filled with a dozen different scenarios, none of them good. And I begin to accept those scenarios as reality when they are anything but! So I need Your help, Lord, to calm my racing heart, rein in my imagination, allay my fears, and lift this darkness hanging over me. I need You, Lord, to be my confidence. Help me to stand firm in You and Your Word when whorls of worries try to overtake me and panic pounces on me. Shine Your light on the recesses of my mind until all shadows dissipate and Your peace fills me once more. In Jesus' name, amen.

Reframing

My sighing comes before my food, and my groanings are poured out like water. For the thing which I greatly fear comes upon me, and that of which I am afraid befalls me. I was not or am not at ease, nor had I or have I rest, nor was I or am I quiet, yet trouble came and still comes [upon me].

JOB 3:24–26 AMPC

Lord, there was once a time when my faith spurred me on to thinking and believing with a certainty that You had put a hedge of protection around me, a hedge that kept me from harm. But then my faith faltered a bit and fear broke in. Now I find myself in a place where exactly the things that I feared have actually come into being, have become a part of my reality. And now I feel lost, restless, and uneasy, and I'm even more afraid of not just my fears but their power, because trouble continues to dog my every step. So I'm running to You, Lord, begging for protection and peace. Help me reframe my thoughts. Help me find a way to banish my fears and build my faith in Jesus. Amen.

Stepping Out

Peter, suddenly bold, said, "Master, if it's really you,
call me to come to you on the water." He said,
"Come ahead." Jumping out of the boat, Peter walked
on the water to Jesus. But when he looked down at the
waves churning beneath his feet, he lost his nerve and
started to sink. He cried, "Master, save me!"

MATTHEW 14:28–30 MSG

There are moments, Jesus, when I have courage and am more than ready for the challenges before me. So I take a bold step forward, knowing that You, Master, have invited me to step out in faith. Eagerly, I take the leap. My feet wet, I walk out to You standing there, waiting for me. But then my focus veers away. My eyes see the waves roiling beneath me. I feel the wind spraying salt water on my face. My vision starts to blur, and the next thing I know, I'm sinking in fear. I cry out for You to save me. And that's what I'm doing right now in this moment, Lord—asking You to give me the strength to turn from my fears and walk forward in faith. Give me the power and peace I need to stay focused on You and You alone. Amen.

Return to Your Rest

The LORD is gracious and righteous; our God is compassionate. The LORD guards the inexperienced; I was helpless, and He saved me. Return to your rest, my soul, for the LORD has been good to you. For You, LORD, rescued me from death, my eyes from tears, my feet from stumbling. I will walk before the LORD in the land of the living.

PSALM 116:5–9 HCSB

When I lose my cool, Lord, I feel so helpless. And following hard on the heels of those feelings of help-lessness are feelings of hopelessness. Experiencing those emotions makes me feel like I'm still a babe in Christ. I have so much growing up to do, it's almost embarrassing. And that steals even more of my peace. Yet I know You, my Protector. You're full of compassion and empathy. When I'm helpless, You reach out and rescue me from death, tears, and stumbles. You are the One who keeps me on my feet. It is through Your love for me, Lord, that my heart finds peace and my soul finds rest. In Jesus' name, amen.

Sidelines

God's amazing grace be with you! God's robust peace!
. . . Stay calm; mind your own business; do your own
job. You've heard all this from us before, but a reminder
never hurts. We want you living in a way that will
command the respect of outsiders, not lying
around sponging off your friends.

1 THESSALONIANS 1:1; 4:11–12 MSG

I don't know where I'd be, Lord, if it weren't for You
and the grace and peace You so willingly pour down
on me. For that peace is just what I need to follow
Your lead, to be an example to others who are walking
Your way. Help me, Lord, to stay calm, to remember
that You love me, will always be here for me, and will
forever care for me. Give me the strength to mind my
own business, to do my own work, to live in such a way
that You and Your Son will be glorified, that people
will see His light instead of me, that He will "move
into the center, while I slip off to the sidelines" (John
3:30 MSG). In Jesus' name, amen.

The Big Help

I will lift up my eyes to the mountains. Where will my help come from? My help comes from the Lord, Who made heaven and earth. He will not let your feet go out from under you. He Who watches over you will not sleep. Listen, He Who watches over Israel will not close his eyes or sleep.

PSALM 121:1–4 NLV

Walking along the road of life, Lord, I often discover that my focus is more on where I'll land than on where I actually am. But You have advised me, Lord, to live in the present, not the future. So today I lift my eyes up to You, Your mountains, Your heights. For You, the Creator and Caretaker of all, are all the help I need. You will not let me trip up. You're the One who watches over me when I sleep. In fact, You, my Defender, never close Your eyes. Be my Lookout, my ever-vigilant Protector. Keep me from losing my way, from losing my courage, from losing my peace. Lord, You are the One who holds me and mine in Your hands forevermore. Amen.

Clear and Open

*I have taught you in the way of skillful and godly
Wisdom [which is comprehensive insight into the ways
and purposes of God]; I have led you in paths of
uprightness. When you walk, your steps shall not
be hampered [your path will be clear and open];
and when you run, you shall not stumble.
Take firm hold of instruction, do not let
go; guard her, for she is your life.*

PROVERBS 4:11–13 AMPC

The more I get to know You, Lord, the more I learn in
Your Word, the more the peace within me grows. For
Your wisdom, instruction, guidance, and direction are
what help me find boundaries, borders, blockages, and
breakthroughs. Just learning Your many names gives me
insight into who You are and who You are growing me
to be—a gentle, patient, strong, and peaceful woman
of God in Christ. So, Lord, as I continue walking along
the way, with You by my side, I know my pathway will
be clear and open. Give me the map You would have
me follow. In Jesus' name, amen.

Fan the Flames of Love

Get along among yourselves, each of you doing your part. . . . Gently encourage the stragglers, and reach out for the exhausted. . . . Be patient with each person, attentive to individual needs. . . . Don't snap at each other. Look for the best in each other, and always do your best to bring it out. Be cheerful no matter what; pray all the time; thank God no matter what happens. This is the way God wants you who belong to Christ Jesus to live.

1 Thessalonians 5:13–18 MSG

One way to maintain my peace, within and without, Lord, is to be like Jesus. But for that, I'll definitely need Your unerring wisdom and supernatural assistance. Help me, Lord, to do that work You've put in my hands to do. Give me words of encouragement to share with people who are exhausted as well as the patience to persevere, allowing people to find their way at their own pace. Most of all, Lord, help me to look for the best in others, not the worst. Help me to find Your light within each human being. Then, Lord, give me the words that will fan their flames of love. In Jesus' name I serve and pray. Amen.

Heart Set

"If you set your heart on God and reach out to him,
if you scrub your hands of sin and refuse to entertain
evil in your home. . . . You'll forget your troubles. . . .
Your world will be washed in sunshine, every shadow
dispersed by dayspring. Full of hope, you'll relax,
confident again; you'll look around, sit back, and take
it easy. Expansive, without a care in the world,
you'll be hunted out by many for your blessing."

JOB 11:13–14, 16–19 MSG

My troubles have been weighing me down, Lord, keeping me anxious, afraid, distracted. I'm so full of worry that I'm neither walking forward or backward. I'm stuck in this one spot. I need hope, Lord—hope that things will get better. That someday all my confusion, woes, and fears will drop away. That peace will then follow. For now, Lord, I'm going to do what I can from my end. I'm setting my heart on and reaching out to You, embracing good and eschewing evil. For when I do, Your Word tells me my troubles will soon be forgotten, as if they never were. As hope will once more reign, I'll be able to relax, take it easy, in You. Amen.

Answers Already on Their Way

This is the confidence (the assurance, the privilege of boldness) which we have in Him: [we are sure] that if we ask anything (make any request) according to His will (in agreement with His own plan), He listens to and hears us. And if (since) we [positively] know that He listens to us in whatever we ask, we also know [with settled and absolute knowledge] that we have. . .the requests made of Him.

1 JOHN 5:14–15 AMPC

It's amazing, Lord, how You walk with me through every situation in my life. How I am never alone but have You, the Creator of the universe, helping me every step of the way. For You have made it clear that if I ask for anything that agrees with Your Word, will, and way, You will not only hear my request but grant it! The certainty of that promise gives me great confidence and peace of mind. So here I am today, Lord, coming to You in prayer. Help me make sure that my requests are aligned with Your desire for me. Then help me rest in assurance, confident that You have heard my requests and that Your answers are already on their way. In Jesus' name I pray. Amen.

Nevertheless

They anointed David king over Israel, according to the
word of the LORD by Samuel. And David and all Israel
went to Jerusalem, that is, Jebus, where the Jebusites
were. . . . The inhabitants of Jebus said to David,
"You will not come in here." Nevertheless, David took
the stronghold of Zion, that is, the city of David. . . .
And David lived in the stronghold; therefore
it was called the city of David.
1 CHRONICLES 11:3–5, 7 ESV

Lord, I refuse to lose my peace. No matter how bad
a situation looks, I know how well and quickly You
can turn things around. No matter how many people
try to dissuade me, force me out, talk over me, or
criticize me, I'm hanging on to You, taking my cues
and confidence from You. Because no matter how bad
or hopeless things may seem or look, I know that for
each one of Your children, You have a "nevertheless"
up Your sleeve. And it's that "nevertheless" I look
for with great anticipation and excitement. In Jesus'
name, amen.

Build Up

*Every wise woman builds her house, but a foolish one
tears it down with her own hands. . . . The heart knows
its own bitterness, and no outsider shares in its joy. . . .
A wise man is cautious and turns from evil, but a fool
is easily angered and is careless. . . . A tranquil heart is
life to the body, but jealousy is rottenness to the bones.*

PROVERBS 14:1, 10, 16, 30 HCSB

There are times, Lord, when I hear myself speak and
find myself wincing in pain. For the words that can
sometimes fly out of my mouth are harmful ones, words
I'm not proud of. They seem to end up tearing others
down instead of building them up. Perhaps there's some
bitterness and unforgiveness I need to deal with. But
in the meantime, Lord, remind me to think before I
speak. Help me not to lose my temper but to make it
my aim to hold nothing but peace and love in my heart.
For then the words that come from my mouth will
help, not hinder, their hearers, including me. Amen.

An Enormous Ask

"Do not worry about your life. Do not worry about
what you are going to eat and drink. Do not worry
about what you are going to wear. Is not life more
important than food? Is not the body more important
than clothes? Look at the birds in the sky. They do
not plant seeds. They do not gather grain. . . .
Yet your Father in heaven feeds them! Are you
not more important than the birds?"
MATTHEW 6:25–26 NLV

Lord, Your Word tells me not to worry about food
and clothing or anything else that's going on (or not
going on) in my life. On some days that feels like an
enormous task. Yet still Your Word stands. And still I
must follow it. So, Lord, every morning, greet me with
a kiss and a good word, one I can carry in my heart and
mind through my day. By midafternoon, Lord, show
me what You would have me do to help another. And
in the evening, Lord, as I lie on my bed, remind me
of my blessings as I fall asleep in Your arms. Amen.

Waiting in Silence

For God alone my soul waits in silence; from Him
comes my salvation. He only is my Rock and my
Salvation, my Defense and my Fortress, I shall not be
greatly moved. . . . My soul, wait only upon God and
silently submit to Him; for my hope and expectation are
from Him. He only is my Rock and my Salvation; He is
my Defense and my Fortress, I shall not be moved.

PSALM 62:1–2, 5–6 AMPC

My patience, Lord, is wearing thin. That means that
hour by hour, day by day, my peace has been leaking
away. Now it's almost gone. And that will not do. So I
come to You today, Lord. My soul waits silently before
You, my Rock and my Savior. Here in Your presence
I can rest. Here I will sit until You speak. For I know
that it is in the deep, deep silence that I will clearly
hear Your voice, Your direction, Your wisdom, Your
answer. You alone can tell me when You are ready for
me to move. And until then, I wait in expectancy and
hope. In You, my supreme fortress, defense, and peace.
In Jesus' name I live and pray. Amen.

Woes in Tow

Keep your foot [give your mind to what you are doing]
when you go. . . .to the house of God. For to draw near
to hear and obey is better than to give the sacrifice of
fools. . . . Be not rash with your mouth, and let not
your heart be hasty to utter a word before God.
For God is in heaven, and you are on earth;
therefore let your words be few.
ECCLESIASTES 5:1–2 AMPC

I have so many things on my mind, Lord, that any
peace I may have had at some point has flown right out
the window. As a result, my focus and concentration
are way off. So I'm making my way back to You, Lord,
with all my woes in tow. I'm going to draw so near
to You that I can hear You breathing and Your heart
beating. Then I'm going to snuggle up and take in the
beauty and wonder of Your presence, the warmth of
Your light, the peace of Your mind. Here, this close
with You, my words will be few but my love abundant.
In Jesus' name, amen.

Beginning Now

*With God rests my salvation and my glory; He is my
Rock of unyielding strength and impenetrable hardness,
and my refuge is in God! Trust in, lean on, rely on,
and have confidence in Him at all times, you people;
pour out your hearts before Him. God is a refuge
for us (a fortress and a high tower). Selah
[pause, and calmly think of that]!*
PSALM 62:7–8 AMPC

I have so many things on my mind, Lord, and they're
sapping me of my strength. For each one carries with
it a potential concern. Yet since concerns are what I'm
not to be focused on, I've been trying to tamp down
all my worries. Unfortunately, today I feel like all
my frets have imploded within me, knocking me off
balance. So I'm running to You, Lord, my high tower.
I'm pouring out to You all the worries that have been
building up inside me, stealing my peace, darkening
my heart. One by one, I leave my woes at Your feet,
beginning right now, in this moment. Amen.

Peace Restored

*May the Lord direct your hearts into [realizing and
showing] the love of God. . . . And as for you,
brethren, do not become weary or lose heart in doing
right [but continue in well-doing without weakening]
. . . . Now may the Lord of peace Himself grant you
His peace (the peace of His kingdom) at all times
and in all ways [under all circumstances and
conditions, whatever comes].*

2 THESSALONIANS 3:5, 13, 16 AMPC

Some days, Lord, I feel so frustrated. I keep putting
love and compassion out there in the world, whenever
and wherever I can, and I often get back nothing but
silence, suspicion, or disdain. I try to live my life as You
would have me live it, doing the right thing, helping
others, but it's hard to stay up and in the light when
so many people are so down and in the dark. That's
why I'm coming to You, Lord, to restore my peace by
asking You to direct my heart toward whom You would
have me help and to leave the results of my efforts to
You. Help me, no matter what my circumstances, to
keep Your peace in me. Amen.

Coming and Going

*The Lord watches over you. The Lord is your safe cover
at your right hand. The sun will not hurt you during the
day and the moon will not hurt you during the night.
The Lord will keep you from all that is sinful. He will
watch over your soul. The Lord will watch over
your coming and going, now and forever.*

PSALM 121:5–8 NLV

❧

I love the idea of You watching over me, Lord, covering
me from all dangers within and without. Because of
You and Your 24-7 vigilance, I need not worry about
being harmed during the day or when I sleep at night.
You are a massive shield of protection that surrounds
me—no matter where I am or who I am with or what
I am doing. I need no special tool, phone, book, com-
puter, or electronic device to call You or reach You.
No, I have a direct line to You through prayer. So
help me keep that in mind, Lord, as I go through my
day. May the idea that You are watching me now and
will do so forever help me not only keep my peace but
revel in it, for You are the source of calm I yearn for.
In Jesus' name, amen.

Breaking Through

David asked the Lord, "Should I go up against
the Philistines? Will You give them into my hand?"
And the Lord said to David, "Go up, for it is sure that
I will give the Philistines into your hand." So David
came to Baal-perazim and beat them there in battle.
He said, "The Lord has broken through those who
hate me like the breaking through of a flood."

2 SAMUEL 5:19–20 NLV

⚜

When people, situations, and things come against
me, Lord, I find myself either cowering in the corner,
speed walking the other way, or physically lashing out
in some way—all before coming to You and asking for
Your advice or help. Then, before I know it, everything,
including me, starts breaking apart and I'm not just
down for the count, but I've lost whatever fragile peace
I started out with, putting me in even more trouble
than before. This time I'm asking You, Lord, what to
do, knowing that with You on my side, nothing can
defeat me or disturb my calm in You. For You break
through all barriers. You protect me from all that comes
against me. You Lord, *are* my breakthrough. Amen.

167

A Solution Unimaginable

*The Philistines came up again. . . . David asked the
Lord what he should do. And the Lord said, "Do not
go up, but go around behind them and come at them in
front of the balsam trees. When you hear the sound
of their steps in the tops of the balsam trees, then hurry
to fight, for then the Lord will have gone out
before you to destroy the Philistine army."
David did just as the Lord told him.*

2 SAMUEL 5:22–25 NLV

❧

Nothing like being challenged once more by the same
old enemy, Lord. And this time, in my uncertainty, I
feel as if I have no firm footing. How many times will
I have to fight the same foe, Lord? When will I ever
regain my peace? And that's when I realize You will
most likely come up with a battle plan or solution I'd
never dreamed or imagined. For Your thoughts and
plans, Lord, are not the same as the thoughts and plans
I entertain. But it *is* in You that I do trust. So here I
come, Lord, asking Your help once more. Tell me what
to do against this latest challenge, and I'll do just as You
say. In Jesus' name, amen.

The True Treasure

*Trust not in and rely confidently not on extortion and
oppression, and do not vainly hope in robbery; if riches
increase, set not your heart on them. God has spoken
once, twice have I heard this: that power belongs
to God. Also to You, O Lord, belong mercy and
loving-kindness, for You render to every
man according to his work.*

PSALM 62:10–12 AMPC

There have been times in my life, Lord, when I've felt
as poor as the proverbial church mouse. Yet, eventually, when things did get better financially, I started
slipping in my walk with You. For I found myself less
in prayer and Your presence and more in strategizing
how to obtain additional money. I began relying on my
"riches" instead of You, Lord. So, Lord who provides
all (Genesis 22:14), I'm once more setting my heart
on You, not riches. For You are the One who holds all
the power in the universe. You are the true treasure
here and beyond. In Jesus' name I pray. Amen.

Quiet Time

"The Lord is in His holy house. Let all the earth be quiet before Him." . . . He who is careful in what he says has much learning, and he who has a quiet spirit is a man of understanding. Even a fool, when he keeps quiet, is thought to be wise. When he closes his lips, he is thought of as a man of understanding. . . . O Lord, put a watch over my mouth. Keep watch over the door of my lips. . . . "Teach me, and I will be quiet. Show me where I have been wrong."

HABAKKUK 2:20; PROVERBS 17:27–28;
PSALM 141:3; JOB 6:24 NLV

So often, Lord, the time I spend in Your presence is perhaps not really prayer. Lately it's been a time during which I pour out my heart and mind to You, then go on my way, do my own thing. No wonder peace has been so elusive for me lately. So help me, Lord, to stop my mental chattering. Pull me close. Let me rest my head against Your chest while I wait, still and silent. Tell me, Lord, what You have to say. Teach me what You'd have me know. Show me what You'd have me see in this quiet time with You. Amen.

Just When You Need It

*We do not have a High Priest Who is unable to
understand and sympathize and have a shared feeling
with our weaknesses and infirmities. . . . Let us then
fearlessly and confidently and boldly draw near to the
throne of grace (the throne of God's unmerited favor to
us sinners), that we may receive mercy [for our failures]
and find grace to help in good time for every need
[appropriate help and well–timed help,
coming just when we need it].*

HEBREWS 4:15–16 AMPC

You, Jesus, know everything about me—my strengths
and weaknesses, my ups and downs, my wins and losses,
my solutions and problems. And You are more than
familiar with all the hurts and hallelujahs that come
into one's life. For You were mocked, betrayed, scorned,
lashed, and tortured. Yet You still held Your peace. No
matter what. That's the peace I want to have, Lord.
As I draw near to You today, Lord, as I approach Your
throne, please give me Your help, mercy, grace, and
peace just when I need it. In Your name, amen.

The First Thing

The first thing I want you to do is pray. Pray every way
you know how, for everyone you know. Pray especially
for rulers and their governments to rule well so we can
be quietly about our business of living simply, in humble
contemplation. This is the way our Savior God wants
us to live. . . . What I want mostly is for men to pray—
not shaking angry fists at enemies but raising holy
hands to God. And I want women to get in
there with the men in humility before God.
1 TIMOTHY 2:1–3, 8–9 MSG

Prayer is such a powerful tool and an essential component of my relationship with You, Lord. For all endeavors, all plans and challenges, seem to begin with words. Good words. Yet I know at times that I'm lax in my duty to pray. Help me change that up now, Lord. To really get back into prayer, conversation with You, and go deep. Help me also, Lord, to pray for *all* people, including politicians, even if I neither respect nor agree with them. For then we believers can live in peace and quiet, going about our day to live and serve You. In Jesus' name, amen.

All My Tomorrows

Deceit is in the heart of those who devise evil, but those
who plan peace have joy. . . . Anxiety in a man's heart
weighs him down, but a good word makes him glad.
PROVERBS 12:20, 25 ESV

You, Lord, are a planner. You know exactly how everything is going to work out for me. Many times I've wished I knew what was going to happen. Yet at other times, I'm glad I cannot see into my future. Regardless of how I feel about knowing or not knowing, You've hidden my tomorrows from me. And as I walk this earth, I'm trusting that You will continue to be with me, for me, and in me. That You will forever be with me, loving and protecting me till the end of time. Because I trust You, I can rest in You. I can put all my tomorrows in Your hands. That leaves me free to plan peace. To find ways that I can becalm others. So plant some good words in my head, Lord. Then tell me who to speak them to so I can plant the peace and spread the joy I find in You. Amen.

Mirroring God's Tranquility

*Every man to whom God has given riches and
possessions, and the power to enjoy them and to accept
his appointed lot and to rejoice in his toil—this is the
gift of God [to him]. For he shall not much remember
[seriously] the days of his life, because God [Himself]
answers and corresponds to the joy of his heart
[the tranquility of God is mirrored in him].*

ECCLESIASTES 5:19–20 AMPC

❧

Too often, Lord, I find that the bad things that are happening in this world are overshadowing the blessings You have given me. That's put me in a very discontented state. That means I need to change my focus and attitude, Lord—and I need to do that right now. But I cannot do so without Your help. For, Lord, I want to do more than just focus on the blessings, all the riches and possessions You've given me, as well as the joys of working in and for You. For what I desire even more, Lord, is to mirror Jesus. To nourish the peace and joy I have in You all the days of my life. In Jesus' name, amen.

Journey at God's Rhythm

Run away from infantile indulgence. Run after mature righteousness—faith, love, peace—joining those who are in honest and serious prayer before God. Refuse to get involved in inane discussions; they always end up in fights. God's servant must not be argumentative, but a gentle listener and a teacher who keeps cool, working firmly but patiently with those who refuse to obey.

2 TIMOTHY 2:22–24 MSG

I see so many people running from here to there, Lord, so fast they cannot catch their breath, nor a glimpse of You. Yet You, Lord, want believers to take their time, to find Your pace, to journey at Your rhythm. But sometimes we need Your help. At least I know I do. So, Lord, help me to turn away from the things that hinder my pursuit of You. And be with me as I run after things of You—faith, love, and peace. Give me the wisdom to avoid mindless arguments, ones in which people do more talking than listening. Above all, Lord, help me be an easy and interested listener to all, staying calm, cool, and collected no matter the words of others. Amen.

A Handful of Quietness

I saw that all toil and all skill in work come from a man's envy of his neighbor. This also is vanity and a striving after wind. The fool folds his hands and eats his own flesh. Better is a handful of quietness than two hands full of toil and a striving after wind.

ECCLESIASTES 4:4–6 ESV

Trying to keep up with the Joneses is exhausting, Lord, and can go on forever. And that's not what I want to spend my life doing, for there's no peace to be found in such a competition. I'd much rather be working for You and striving for the things You want me to reach for, things such as peace, courage, patience, love, forgiveness, and compassion. So help me, Lord, to strike a balance between using my hands to meet the needs of the flesh and the needs of the spirit. And as I do so, Lord, help me to be more content with a handful of quietness in Your presence than clutching all the work I can handle with my only gain afterward being a fleeting pleasure soon blown away with the wind. Amen.

Slow to Anger

Then the LORD passed in front of him and proclaimed:
Yahweh—Yahweh is a compassionate and gracious God,
slow to anger and rich in faithful love and truth. . . .
Tear your hearts, not just your clothes, and return
to the LORD your God. For He is gracious and
compassionate, slow to anger, rich in faithful
love. . . . A hot-tempered man stirs up conflict,
but a man slow to anger calms strife.
EXODUS 34:6; JOEL 2:13; PROVERBS 15:18 HCSB

You, Lord, are a God of peace. That was seen in a big
way when You allowed Your Son to be killed so that I
could live with and love You forever. That's an *amazing*
amount of compassion and love You have shown for
Your oftentimes wayward children. Yet that's exactly
the kind of peace, love, and compassion I want in my
own life. I want to be a woman slow to anger, someone
who doesn't create but calms the strife around me.
Protect me, Lord, as I endeavor to be like You. Amen.

Getting Along

Work at getting along with each other and with God.
Otherwise you'll never get so much as a glimpse of God.
Make sure no one gets left out of God's generosity.
Keep a sharp eye out for weeds of bitter discontent.
A thistle or two gone to seed can ruin a whole garden
in no time. Watch out for the Esau syndrome:
trading away God's lifelong gift in order
to satisfy a short-term appetite.
HEBREWS 12:14–16 MSG

❧

Lord, I want to live a life where I not only get along with people but go the extra mile to help them. You emphasize that I am to love You with all I am and love others as I love myself. You have created love to be Your children's pathway to peace. And that's the road I want to be on. But some people, Lord, are a bit hard to love. So please fill my heart with love, my soul with peace, and my lips with encouraging words as I reach out to all around me, in honor of Your Son, Jesus. Amen.

Falling into Peace

The Lord weighs the spirits (the thoughts and intents of the heart). Roll your works upon the Lord [commit and trust them wholly to Him; He will cause your thoughts to become agreeable to His will, and] so shall your plans be established and succeed. . . . When a man's ways please the Lord, He makes even his enemies to be at peace with him.

PROVERBS 16:2–3, 7 AMPC

Lord, I come to You today in quiet contemplation. Within myself, Lord, I feel some discord. So I come before You looking for love, comfort, and ease. Please weigh the intents of my thoughts and heart. Here are my plans. . . . My prayer is that You would consider my ideas and aims. Then give me a sign of Your approval or disapproval. For I want to make sure my proposed ways are aligned with Your way for me. I want my thoughts to agree with Yours. For only then will my plans succeed, only then will things fall into peace and place. Your thoughts, Lord? Amen.

Unanxious and Unintimidated

What matters is not your outer appearance. . .but your inner disposition. Cultivate inner beauty, the gentle, gracious kind that God delights in. The holy women of old were beautiful before God that way, and were good, loyal wives to their husbands. Sarah, for instance, taking care of Abraham, would address him as "my dear husband." You'll be true daughters of Sarah if you do the same, unanxious and unintimidated.

1 PETER 3:3–6 MSG

How freeing it is, Lord, knowing that You aren't concerned with my outer appearance, that I don't have to dress up to impress or please You. For that's only surface beauty. But I do need Your guidance in how to be beautiful on the inside. So, lead me, Lord, to the verses that will guide me to a place at rest in You. There I will sit at Your feet and take in Your wisdom. There, Lord, teach me how to be at ease, confident, and unintimidated. Teach me how to be just like Jesus. In His name I pray. Amen.

The God of Peace

Now may the God of peace, who brought up from the
dead our Lord Jesus—the great Shepherd of the sheep—
with the blood of the everlasting covenant, equip you
with all that is good to do His will, working in us
what is pleasing in His sight, through Jesus Christ.
Glory belongs to Him forever and ever. Amen.
HEBREWS 13:20–21 HCSB

Part of my peace, Lord, comes from knowing that whatever You call me to You will also equip me for. And it's all because You are the God of peace, because You stop all the turmoil, assuage my fear, strengthen me against temptation, and fight for me against troublemakers. It is You, Lord—who had the supreme power to raise Jesus from the dead—who gives me the *real* rest, the true rest I need to take in You. It is while I rest in You and Your peace, in Your power and Your strength, that You do even more work within me. Thank You, Lord, for all the good You do me. Amen.

Every Hour

And then he prayed, "God, I'm asking for two things
before I die; don't refuse me—Banish lies from my lips
and liars from my presence. Give me enough food
to live on, neither too much nor too little. If I'm
too full, I might get independent, saying, 'God?
Who needs him?' If I'm poor, I might steal
and dishonor the name of my God."

PROVERBS 30:7–9 MSG

You know the needs I have, Lord, as well as my desires
to be worry-free, to acquire a gentle and peaceful
mien. To that end, Lord, keep me honest at the core.
And help me see beyond the lies of others. Wherever
needed, Lord, unveil the truth so that I can find my
way through this maze of life on earth. Yet also, Lord, I
ask for enough food to live on each day. Not too much
and not too little. Just enough to be nourished but not
so much that I get cocky and determine I don't need
You anymore. For the truth is, Lord, that I need You.
Every hour. From now until eternity. Amen.

What "Works"

What good is it, my brothers, if someone says he has faith but does not have works? Can his faith save him? If a brother or sister is without clothes and lacks daily food and one of you says to them, "Go in peace, keep warm, and eat well," but you don't give them what the body needs, what good is it? In the same way faith, if it doesn't have works, is dead by itself.

JAMES 2:14–17 HCSB

Lord, You have given me so much peace across the years that now I want to spread that peace, that calm, that assurance one can find only in You. I want to add works to my faith by helping others. But I'm not sure what those "works" might be. So I'm coming to You for help, for inspiration. Show me, Lord, what You would have me do, how You would have me serve You by coming alongside someone else. Show me where to begin. Give me the courage to reach out. In the meantime, I'll continue to pray and seek Your will, Your way, with my eyes wide open. In Jesus' name I pray. Amen.

Taking It In

"Job, are you listening? Have you noticed all this? Stop in your tracks! Take in God's miracle-wonders!". . . . I look up at your macro-skies, dark and enormous, your handmade sky-jewelry, moon and stars mounted in their settings.

JOB 37:14; PSALM 8:3 MSG

Today, Lord, I have discord within and without, and I'm not sure why. There's really nothing I can put my finger on as the cause of this unease, but the feeling is there nevertheless. So I'm going to follow Your wisdom, Lord, which begins by opening up not just my mind but my ears. There's been so much chattering in my mind, Lord, that it's no wonder I feel a bit disconnected at times. So I'm looking to open my eyes as well, within and without, to see what's around me. I'm going to stop all activity—working, playing, thinking, dreaming—and take in and appreciate all the beauty You have created, all the miracles You've wrought, all the universe You sustain, all the love and light You pour upon me. In Jesus' name, amen.

By Faith

Now faith is the assurance (the confirmation, the title deed) of the things [we] hope for, being the proof of things [we] do not see and the conviction of their reality [faith perceiving as real fact what is not revealed to the senses]. . . . By faith we understand that the worlds. . . were framed. . .by the word of God, so that what we see was not made out of things which are visible.

HEBREWS 11:1, 3 AMPC

When stress knocks on my door, I soon find my faith taking a walkabout. An instant later, my peace is running after it. Then I'm left feeling like a quivering bowl of lime Jell-O, shaking with doubts and anxieties. Lord, this is not at all how You want me to live. So, Lord, fill me with Your presence as I slowly take this next breath and another and another. As I seek You within, Lord, reveal Yourself, Your light, Your warmth, Your love. Remind me that all is well. That You will never leave or forsake me. That all I hope for is already on its way to me through You, my Lord and Savior. My hope and stay. Amen.

The Peace of Obedience

God's Word came to Jonah, Amittai's son: "Up on
your feet and on your way to the big city of Nineveh!
Preach to them. They're in a bad way and I can't
ignore it any longer." But Jonah got up and went the
other direction to Tarshish, running away from God.
He. . .found a ship headed for Tarshish. He. . .went
on board, joining those going to Tarshish—as far
away from God as he could get. But God. . .

JONAH 1:1–4 MSG

I'm feeling a bit like Jonah, Lord. You asked me to do
something somewhere and I didn't do it. Instead of
following Your call, heeding Your direction, I went
the opposite way. I ran from You, going as far away
as I could get emotionally, spiritually, and mentally.
But then You started to take action, to pull me back
onto the right path. Ever since then, Lord, nothing
has gone smoothly for me. I have no peace. So here
I am before You, Lord, ready to listen and obey, to do
what You would have me do. Here I have peace. The
peace obedience to You brings. Amen.

Sweet Peace

*Wherever you find jealousy and fighting, there will be
trouble and every other kind of wrong-doing. But the
wisdom that comes from heaven is first of all pure.
Then it gives peace. It is gentle and willing to obey.
It is full of loving-kindness and of doing good. It has
no doubts and does not pretend to be something
it is not. Those who plant seeds of peace
will gather what is right and good.*

JAMES 3:16–18 NLV

I need some pointers, Lord, on how to make good decisions. In the past, I have talked to family members, partners, coworkers, and friends about what I should do, where I should go, how I should serve. But I still feel so very lost, not quite sure where my true path is. Perhaps, Lord, I've been looking for advice in all the wrong places. Instead of asking my fellow humans, I should be asking You for advice. So here I am, Lord, looking for Your knowledge, for that perfect heavenly wisdom that not only gives me peace but prompts me to plant seeds of peace. Ah, sweet peace, free of fears and worries, is Your wisdom and way. Amen.

Name Calling

"Woman," Jesus said to her, "why are you crying?
Who is it you are looking for?" Supposing He was the
gardener, she replied, "Sir, if you've removed Him, tell
me where you've put Him, and I will take Him away."
Jesus said, "Mary." Turning around, she said to Him
in Hebrew, "Rabbouni!"—which means "Teacher."
JOHN 20:15–16 HCSB

❧

Lord, I have had days when I couldn't find You. When wherever I looked, all our old familiar places seemed empty, bereft of Your presence, light, grace, love, kindness, and direction. I didn't know where to turn, how to reach You. I thought perhaps You were wearing a disguise. Or, much more likely, there was something wrong with my vision. My perception was off. Regardless of the reason, my peace was disturbed and my tears were about to flow. That's when I heard a voice ask, "Why is it you're crying? Who are you looking for?" And my answer was "Tell me where Jesus is. And I'll take Him away with me." Next thing I knew, You were calling my name. I heard and felt the love in Your voice. The scales fell away and it was You I saw before me. Peace and joy once more were mine. Amen.

Standing on the Shore

Simon Peter announced, "I'm going fishing."
The rest of them replied, "We're going with you."
They went out and got in the boat. They caught nothing
that night. When the sun came up, Jesus was standing
on the beach, but they didn't recognize him. . . .
He said, "Throw the net off the right side of the boat
and see what happens." They did what he said.
All of a sudden there were so many fish in it,
they weren't strong enough to pull it in.

JOHN 21:3–4, 6 MSG

When I'm restless, anxious, afraid, impatient, confused, or frustrated, Lord, I find myself automatically going back to something familiar, something from my old life that once brought me comfort, hoping to regain my peace. Yet I soon discover that whenever I attempt anything without You, I come up empty. No matter how hard or how long I try or how much help I have, my endeavor without You bears no fruit. But then You appear on the scene, standing on the shore. You see me floundering in the sea. You, who appear to me a stranger, yell instructions. I obey. And my efforts pay off, big-time! That's when I realize it's *You* standing on the shore. *You* are my blessing. *You* are my peace. *You* are my bounty. Amen.

Being a Blessing

Now finally, all of you should be like-minded
and sympathetic, should love believers, and be
compassionate and humble, not paying back evil
for evil or insult for insult but, on the contrary,
giving a blessing, since you were called for this,
so that you can inherit a blessing.

1 PETER 3:8–9 HCSB

❧

On the whole, Lord, I'm not a very vengeful person, looking to hurt others, to pay them back for any wrong they did me. But I definitely need Your help in forgiving them. Lord, give me the courage to turn the other cheek, go the extra mile, give in addition to what has been taken. Some people may say that makes me a light touch, a patsy. I say it makes me more like You, Jesus—and a true person of peace. A person who sees others with compassion and love, who wants to help make the lives of others better. Lord, I want to be a blessing to all I meet. That sounds like a very tall order, but You have said that with You, I can do anything. So let's begin today, Lord. Who can I bless in Jesus' name? Amen.

A Shadow amid
the Darkness

Keep awake! Watch at all times. The devil is working
against you. He is walking around like a hungry lion
with his mouth open. He is looking for someone to
eat. Stand against him and be strong in your faith.
Remember, other Christians over all the world are
suffering the same as you are. After you have suffered
for awhile, God Himself will make you perfect. He will
keep you in the right way. He will give you strength.

1 Peter 5:8–10 nlv

Sometimes, Lord, I forget what I'm up against. That
there is a liar, a shadow amid the darkness, a devil
working against me. Your description of him walking
around like a ravenous lion with his jaw open gnaws
at my peace a bit. But then I remember who You are.
That with You I can stand against that devil and be
strong in my faith. That other Christians around the
world are suffering along with me, if not more. Yet
still, You are with me, making me perfect, keeping me
on the right path, giving me strength, and most of all,
filling me with Your abundant peace. Amen.

Walk Steadily

*By faith Enoch was taken up so that he should not see
death, and he was not found, because God had taken
him. Now before he was taken he was commended as
having pleased God. And without faith it is impossible
to please him, for whoever would draw near to
God must believe that he exists and that
he rewards those who seek him.*

HEBREWS 11:5–6 ESV

❧

Lord, as I draw near to You today, I have great peace
and expectations. For You have said that whoever
comes near You needs to believe You are real, not just
a panacea for the masses. To me You *are* more real and
true than the chair on which I sit, the desk on which
I write, the phone on which I talk. And I want to
walk with You just as Enoch did so many thousands
of years ago. Because he walked steadily with You,
Lord, You just took him one day (Genesis 5:21–24).
He was simply gone from the earth. What a reward!
As I draw near to You today, Lord, show me what I
can do to please You. Amen.

Every Kind of Peace

She [your sister church here] in Babylon, [who is] elect (chosen) with [yourselves], sends you greetings, and [so does] my son (disciple) Mark. Salute one another with a kiss of love [the symbol of mutual affection]. To all of you that are in Christ Jesus (the Messiah), may there be peace (every kind of peace and blessing, especially peace with God, and freedom from fears, agitating passions, and moral conflicts). Amen (so be it).

1 PETER 5:13–14 AMPC

That's what I want and need, Lord. Every kind of peace. For every situation. For every moment I live and breathe. I want peace within and without. I want peace to grow up in You. I want peace to fall upon people everywhere on this earth so that there will be more kindness than cruelty. So that wars will cease. So that children can go to school without being afraid. Lord, most of all, I want peace with You and freedom from fears. No more conflict, no more tension, no more stress, no more angst. Help me find every kind of peace, Lord, within and without, and then pass it on. In Jesus' name, amen.

Eyes on the Lord

*Because Moses had faith, he would not be called the
son of Pharaoh's daughter when he grew up. He chose
to suffer with God's people instead of having fun doing
sinful things for awhile. Any shame that he suffered for
Christ was worth more than all the riches in Egypt.
He kept his eyes on the reward God was going to give
him. Because Moses had faith, he left Egypt. He was
not afraid of the king's anger. Moses did not turn from
the right way but kept seeing God in front of him.*

HEBREWS 11:24–27 NLV

Lord, Moses wasn't perfect—and neither am I. That's
not a boast, just a fact. Yet it's a good fact, because
Moses' story proves that even fallible human beings
like me can become great heroes of faith. So here I
am, Lord. My eye is on the reward You have waiting
for me. And because You are with me as I walk down
this road of life, I'm rewarded with the peace I can
find only in You, Lord. And because of Your presence
and Your peace, I am not afraid of anyone's anger or
power. All I do is keep my eyes on You, Lord, as You
walk in front of me, going before me, one step, one
day at a time. Amen.

Ultimate Peace

Shadrach, Meshach, and Abednego replied to the king,
"Nebuchadnezzar, . . . If the God we serve exists,
then He can rescue us from the furnace of blazing fire,
and He can rescue us from the power of you, the king.
But even if He does not rescue us, we want you as
king to know that we will not serve your gods
or worship the gold statue you set up."

DANIEL 3:16–18 HCSB

Talk about the ultimate peace! That's what Shadrach, Meshach, and Abednego demonstrated when King Nebuchadnezzar had them thrown into a fiery furnace because they wouldn't bow to his statue. They calmly told the king that God could rescue them, not only from the furnace but from the enraged king *and* his power! So they retained their peace of mind, telling Nebuchadnezzar that even if God decided not to rescue them, they would never bow down to any of his gods! Next thing the men knew, they were trussed up and thrown into an extra-hot furnace. Yet within that same furnace, a fourth man appeared who looked "like a son of the gods" (Daniel 3:25 HCSB). That's the kind of faith and peace I want, Lord. One in which peace reigns and Jesus appears. Amen.

At Home Once More

The Scripture says, No man who believes in Him
[who adheres to, relies on, and trusts in Him] will
[ever] be put to shame or be disappointed. [No one]
for there is no distinction. . . . The same Lord is
Lord over all [of us] and He generously bestows
His riches upon all who call upon Him [in faith].
For everyone who calls upon the name of the
Lord [invoking Him as Lord] will be saved.

ROMANS 10:11–13 AMPC

When I'm down-and-out, fuming and frustrated, alone
and abused, concerned and confused, I reach out for
You, Lord. In faith, I seek Your presence, Your power,
Your touch, Your love, Your strength, Your protection,
and Your peace. All seems elusive. My thoughts remain unfocused. And then I remember the power of
You, Jesus, the power of Your name. I clear my head
and throat and then say, "Jesus. . .Jesus. . .Jesus." At
the sound of Your name, my agitation begins to fade.
I find my footing, my peace, my Lord. Once more
in Your presence, I am whole and at home. In Your
name, amen.

A Good Look

*Do not judge and criticize and condemn others, so that
you may not be judged and criticized and condemned
yourselves. For just as you judge and criticize and
condemn others, you will be judged and criticized
and condemned, and in accordance with the
measure you [use to] deal out to others,
it will be dealt out again to you.*

MATTHEW 7:1–2 AMPC

Oftentimes, Lord, You tell me through Your Word
that I'll reap what I sow. That whenever I judge and
criticize others, I too will be judged and criticized.
Help me keep this in mind, Lord, when I come to
You complaining that I've lost my peace. For that's
when I need to take a good look at myself, to consider
when I may have picked on others, pointed out their
failures, and picked at their faults. For it may be that
that critical spirit with which I attacked others may
have just attached itself to me, sucking all the peace
out of my life. Help me replace my critical attitude,
Lord, with one of encouragement and praise. Help me
find and bring out the best in all. In Jesus' name, amen.

Stand Amazed

The LORD is merciful and gracious, slow to anger and abounding in steadfast love. He will not always chide, nor will he keep his anger forever. He does not deal with us according to our sins, nor repay us according to our iniquities. For as high as the heavens are above the earth, so great is his steadfast love toward those who fear him; as far as the east is from the west, so far does he remove our transgressions from us.

PSALM 103:8–12 ESV

When I think about how much You love me, Lord, I stand amazed at Your patience, tolerance, and compassion. For I am a woman who has at times given in to temptation, entertained a doubt or two, and definitely made mistakes here and there. Yet still I have peace, because Your Word tells me that You, Lord, have an amazing amount of mercy and grace. You are slow to get angry and have loads of love. Even more amazing, Lord, is that You don't deal with me like I deserve. Instead, You have limitless love for me, so much so that You separate me from my mistakes. In You and Your love, I stand amazed. Amen.

Keeping On

*Keep on asking and it will be given you; keep on seeking
and you will find; keep on knocking [reverently] and
[the door] will be opened to you. For everyone who
keeps on asking receives; and he who keeps on
seeking finds; and to him who keeps on
knocking, [the door] will be opened.*

MATTHEW 7:7–8 AMPC

Lord, I have a feeling I am not as persistent as I could and should be when it comes to prayer requests. It seems I get too easily frustrated and impatient if an answer does not land on my doorstep a day or two after my prayer. Soon disappointment and doubts begin to darken my door and disturb my peace. So it's time to change things up, Lord, to pray as You instruct. From here on, I'm going to ask and keep on asking, seek and keep on seeking, knock and keep on knocking, day after day. And I will do so knowing that I *will* receive what I ask for, *find* what I seek, and see the door that I've been knocking on *open*. Amen.

A Wise Woman

"Everyone then who hears these words of mine and does them will be like a wise man who built his house on the rock. And the rain fell, and the floods came, and the winds blew and beat on that house, but it did not fall, because it had been founded on the rock. And everyone who hears these words of mine and does not do them will be like a foolish man who built his house on the sand. And the rain fell, and the floods came, and the winds blew and beat against that house, and it fell, and great was the fall of it."

MATTHEW 7:24–27 ESV

Lord, part of my walk with You is about not just *hearing* Your words but *taking some action* to live them. For I want to be a wise woman, to construct my house, my life, on the solid rock of Your Word. When I build on Your foundation, my life won't be toppled by wind and water. Please give me some guidance, Lord, as to what words of Yours I should write on my heart and mind at this moment in time. What wisdom do You have for me to partake of today and forever? Amen.

God's Peace Parameters

May grace (God's favor) and peace (which is perfect well-being, all necessary good, all spiritual prosperity, and freedom from fears and agitating passions and moral conflicts) be multiplied to you in [the full, personal, precise, and correct] knowledge of God and of Jesus our Lord. For His divine power has bestowed upon us all things that [are requisite and suited] to life and godliness.

2 PETER 1:2–3 AMPC

∾

I am so grateful, Lord, for the peace You have waiting for me every morning when I awaken, throughout my day, and into the good night. For Your peace is no ordinary peace. Your peace is the feeling of perfect well-being, that I have all the necessary good and all the spiritual prosperity I could ever dream of or imagine. Your peace is a freedom from all fears and disturbing passions I might entertain. But even more wonderful is that Your peace frees me from all moral conflicts. The fact and promise that this peace will be multiplied to me is a wonder-filled blessing. No words can thank You enough, Lord, for pouring Your peace on me. In Jesus' name, amen.

Restoring Peace

*As a father shows compassion to his children,
so the LORD shows compassion to those who fear him.
For he knows our frame; he remembers that we are
dust. As for man, his days are like grass; he flourishes
like a flower of the field; for the wind passes over it,
and it is gone, and its place knows it no more.*

PSALM 103:13–16 ESV

Lord, You know how weak I am. You know that human creatures such as I only live for so long. So please show compassion to me, Lord. Restore my peace by forgiving me where I have fallen short, giving me a hand up when I stumble, filling me with strength when I need it, balancing my frame when I am unsteady, and granting me joy when my heart is aching. In all these ways and for all my days, care for me, Father God. Then give me the power to care for others as I walk Your way and follow Your path. Amen.

God with Me

Look! God's dwelling is with humanity, and He will live with them. They will be His people, and God Himself will be with them and be their God. He will wipe away every tear from their eyes. Death will no longer exist; grief, crying, and pain will exist no longer, because the previous things have passed away.

REVELATION 21:3–4 HCSB

Sometimes, Lord, the idea of death frightens me, disturbing my peace, putting me off balance. Yet then I remember how things will be in the end. You will be living with us. We will be Your people and You will be our God. With Your gentle hand, You promise to wipe away all tears from our eyes. Death will no longer be a part of our reality, nor will grief, crying, and pain. All those things will have passed away, but we will remain in and with You, our light, our love, our hope, our Savior. The idea and hope of You awaiting me at the end of my time on earth restores my peace of mind and brings a smile to my face. For my joy and peace are wrapped up in You, my God. Amen.

Blessed with Peace

The voice of the Lord makes the hinds bring forth their young, and His voice strips bare the forests, while in His temple everyone is saying, Glory! The Lord sat as King over the deluge; the Lord [still] sits as King [and] forever! The Lord will give [unyielding and impenetrable] strength to His people; the Lord will bless His people with peace.

PSALM 29:9–11 AMPC

Your voice, Lord, is the power behind all creation. You spoke and things came into being. You breathed and I came into being, in Your image, in Your love. Your voice still brings forth young, strips trees, and moves mountains. And as King here, in Your temple, You continue to reign and give strength to Your children. But even more wonderful, Lord, is that You have blessed Your people with peace. Help me, Lord, to hang on to the ways and wonder of peace. To pass it along when I can. To pray it down upon this land. To cherish it forever and ever in Jesus' name. Amen.

Scripture Index